C000040949

The Art of Language

The Words we speak can make or break us

Published by

Kima Global Publishers
50, Clovelly Road,
Clovelly
7975
South Africa

First edition October 2016

© Mo Khalpey 2016

ISBN 978-1-920535-99-5
eISBN 978-1-928234-00-5

Publisher's web site: www.kimabooks.com
Author's web site: www.aistiq.com

World rights Kima Global Publishers. No part of this publication may be reproduced, translated, adapted, stored or transmitted in any form or through any means including information storage and retrieval systems without permission in writing from the publisher except for brief excerpts quoted for review purposes.

The Art of Language

The Words We Speak can Make or Break Us

by

Mo Khalpey

Dedication

This book is dedicated in loving memory of my best friend the late Kevin Kistensamy who passed away before the completion of this book. His loyal friendship of thirty one years, dedicated support and encouragement will always be remembered.

Acknowledgements

A special acknowledgement to my dear friend Vianola Makan who's dedicated support and encouragement was my inspiration during the difficult times while writing this book. Another special acknowledgement to a dear friend Saadiya Kathrada who's support and friendship has been the encouragement to getting this material complete after many years of research. A special acknowledgement to all of those who had given their time for me to coach them and providing their constant feedback for the research necessary for the material contained in this book.

A very special acknowledgment to my dearest parents, although thousands of miles away, my gratitude for your emotional support can never be expressed in words.

Mo Khalpey

Note to Reader

The information contained in this book is largely based on my own personal research and experiences. As well as observations of client's experiences whom I have had the opportunity to coach over a period of six years. Although there has been some tremendous or significant success with the coaching and some of the techniques shared here, most of the success has come from the willingness of participants to fully practice what they have been taught.

This success also differs from person to person, as each individual has their own unique personalities and traits. The individuals were personally coached and would share their feedback on a regular basis. It is for this reason that the information contained in this book cannot be guaranteed to work for everyone.

The information here is merely a guide to help you but the success of it will depend on your willingness to practice the techniques as it has been described. However the outcomes of the practicing of the techniques cannot be guaranteed as you the reader are practicing it from the information in this book and are not receiving personal one on one coaching.

Most people who come from fairly stable backgrounds will gain some significant transformation through the practice of these techniques, however this will also vary from person to person, therefore the actual or type of outcomes cannot be guaranteed. Any individual who has come from difficult backgrounds or situations may not gain full benefit from these teachings and may need to work with a coach.

People suffering with psychological disorders or have some trauma from the past, whom have not as yet had any treatment or therapy from professional consolers, may not gain any benefit from this information. Those who have had counselling and are in a stable condition right now can use this information as an added tool but may need to check in with their therapist with regards to dealing with past emotions and situations. Therefore the information here cannot be guaranteed to work for these individuals.

The Author, his affiliates and publishers cannot be held liable in any way should individuals not gain any benefit or positive outcomes as a result of reading or practicing the information or techniques taught here.

Table of Contents

Preface

For many years I have been observing how suggestions placed onto the subconscious mind, through hypnosis, transforms behaviour. I have observed how behaviour can be modified especially if the individual is willing to be persistent with the practice.

I have also observed through the practice of NLP how creating choice can empower a person through the words that they speak and the way they can also transform the way they feel in minutes. I have also had the opportunity to observe how using meditation can help with that transformation.

Meditation is a powerful way of getting the mind clear and the body relaxed. I realised that most people turn away from meditation as they believe it to be something that is for spiritual or religious purposes only.

This is far from the truth. Through my studies of the different form of meditations and knowledge gained through hypnotherapy, I found that meditation can be used for achieving your goals as well. I describe this scientific approach combined with the ancient art of meditation in my book "Aistiq Meditations: A scientific Approach to Achieving Goals"[1].

Observing those who practiced these meditation techniques, I was also able to put together how language plays an important role in transformation. There have

1   Kima Global Publishers 2015

also been many scientific studies around the world on how language actually affects us as human beings.

Through studying this and really listening to how people speak, I realised that people struggled because they were not understanding how the words they were speaking, whether it was to themselves or others, was actually affecting their lives, like a self-fulfilling prophecy.

I wanted to understand why so many people were struggling with this behavioural change despite there being thousands of books and coaches out there all teaching different aspects of self-development. I realised that there was no problems with the techniques being taught, it was resistance that most human beings face either from an unconscious level or the unwillingness to transform oneself because of how difficult it is to deal with oneself.

Through this observation I realised that the most important aspect that was missing in people's lives was that of unconditional self-love. There is great difficulty in getting to that point of self-love because of what people were dealing with. I wanted to understand this from a non-spiritual or religious perspective.

I am not at any point putting down any religion, spiritual group or culture, and I wanted to understand the importance of self-love from a purely human aspect. I also wanted to understand from a non-religious or spiritual perspective why the art of forgiveness was so powerful in transforming people's lives.

When I began to experience for myself how kind words to myself was causing a shift in my thinking and helping me create a positive language, my life started to transform in ways that I could not explain at the time. I became interested in how language affects us some years ago and why it is so important for us to be aware of that.

I quickly realised that people did not need new self-help techniques as thousands of really powerful techniques already exist. My aim was to offer a message that would help people understand in a simple way why they were resisting and struggling with transforming and to achieve their goals despite having learnt so many different techniques.

I realised through my observations and coaching that people don't need to be told what to do, they just need to be guided to understand that they have choice, it is through this choice that they can create the life they want. We don't need to fix other people's problems, they have the power to do it themselves, and they have to make that choice for themselves.

When you transform yourself through self-love, forgiveness and the language that you speak, people will automatically transform to accommodate you. When you transform yourself the world transforms for you. It is for this reason why this book has been written in a way where I don't give you all the answers but lead you to that point of choice and realisation that you have the power and all the answers with you.

Some of the chapters are left open ended so that you can get to those answers through your own internal power which will be more beneficial to you than being told exactly what to do.

However for all of this to happen, we have to let go of our past and detach from it emotionally so that we have the space and power to create the life we really want. It is for this reason I included the chapter with a step by step instruction on how to break those emotions.

I further added techniques that will help you get to the theta level of the subconscious that will help you transform faster. I also had observed how visualization and handwriting is a language of the subconscious mind and added instructional chapters to help you along.

Nothing works until you make it happen by practicing what you learn in the correct way. Only you have the power to create your transformation and until you take that responsibility, you will struggle to achieve those transformations.

To truly help others there has to first be a transformation within yourself. Only then will you have the real power to make a difference in the lives of others. The encouragement to write this book in the way that I did was firstly through the success I experienced from changing my own language, detaching emotionally from my past and most important learning and applying the art of forgiveness and self-love.

Secondly it was through the transformations I observed in others who I have had the privilege to coach. The techniques are so simple, and life can be so simple. It is the exaggerated stories and the unwillingness to let go that makes it so difficult. I hope that the information contained here will encourage you to transform your life into the amazing and powerful life and person you deserve to be. Remember even when working with self-development, you can have fun while doing it, so just enjoy every moment of your journey of self-transformation.

Life is too good to stop now.

Mo Khalpey

Foreword

The Art of Language by Mo Khalpey clearly highlights an area of your life which you take for granted. You are so unaware of how the words you speak have an effect on your subconscious mind that can influence the outcome in your life, whether it is your internal language or spoken to others.

Mo defines this in a way that is simple for you to understand. He has written this book in a way that guides you to finding your own power words that resonate with your subconscious programming. You will understand that you have the power of choice and that the solutions to your obstacles in life actually exist within you.

This is not a book about a new self-help technique but a simple guide to enhancing what you already know through the words that you speak. The words that you speak in the context sentences that you use in everyday language have a tendency to be a self-fulfilling prophecy, making problems in your life look much bigger than what they really are.

Usually when you have an emotional attachment to a negative event from your past, it is the exaggerated story of that negative event that causes the emotional attachment, blocking you from moving forward in life. This is why your past will keep showing up in your future. Whenever you start something for positive transformation, the reason why it seems so difficult is due to subconscious resistance. You will learn to overcome subconscious resistance and procrastination with simple yet effective techniques.

Foreword

Mo provides simple yet effective techniques to understand your subconscious language and to change it for positive transformation. He has also added some basic techniques to overcome your emotional attachments that cause the blocks and obstacles in your life. This book is a 'must read' if you really want to break through the blocks that prevent you from effectively modifying your habits and behaviours, enabling you to access your true power and the patterns that will move you forward in achieving your goals and dreams.

You will start to experience how changing your words and context sentences about yourself will free you to create the transformation you really want.

Raymond Aaron

New York Times Bestselling Author

Introduction

The Art of Language has got nothing to do with what your mother tongue may be or the number of languages you may speak. It has nothing to do with languages whether it is English, French, German, Zulu or anything else. It is about the words that we speak to ourselves which can positively or negatively influence our outcomes in our life, goals and dreams.

Most people don't realise just how powerful words are, whether it may be one single word or in a context sentence. Words can affect us on the subconscious level, an area of mind which most of the time we have very little or no control. There are times when the single words or context sentences of others can negatively affect us, especially in our childhood and teenage years without even being aware of it.

There are times when we make conscious decisions based on the negative subconscious influence of the words of others through the early years to mid-twenties of our lives, generally we are not even aware of this. The effect of these words during our early years can be a negative influence throughout our entire life, preventing us from being able to see our true potential or believing that we have the ability to achieve so much more no matter what our circumstances may be in any given moment.

It does not end there, the words that we speak to ourselves, the self-talk, can negatively or positively influence our outcomes. Sometimes we may believe that we are speaking in a positive tone or language but don't realise that there could be one or more words in those sentences that could be creating the negative outcomes from an unconscious level.

It is this self-talk that influences the way we achieve goals or dreams, the way we tackle obstacles and overcome challenges. All of this can be influenced by single words or a context of a sentence without us even knowing it. Most people don't even realise that their own internal conversations that go on in their heads can make problems look much bigger than what they really are.

The internal self-talk that is constantly going on in our heads are the barriers that hold us back from achieving much more than what we believe to be truly possible. There are times when we are unaware that our internal conversations are showing up in different ways externally in our lives.

We as human beings are so oblivious to this internal self-talk that we fail to see or recognise just how negatively our lives are influenced. How many times have you heard the words "you are your own obstacle" or "it is only you standing in your own way"? Think about it, how true those words are? Nothing can influence you unconsciously more than the words or sentences that you speak to yourself. This is a reality that we are so unaware of most of our life.

Here is something for you to think about; and really think about this for a few minutes and see how it resonates with you. The reality is that there are no such things as failure. The only failure that exists is the conversations about failure going on inside your head. The other existence of failure is your failure to be in action. The truth is that it is not just about doing the things necessary to get what you want but about being what you want to be. We are not human doings, we are human beings. So be and it will be. What are you? Are you a human doing? Or are you a human being?

Look closely and you will realise that in this moment you are a human doing. It is only when you have the courage to break out of your current mould that blocks you from being great, it is only when you have the courage to be what you declare yourself to be, no matter what others may think or say about you, will you truly break all boundaries.

It is then and only then will you usually experience and express being a human being. Change or transformation in your life needs courage, the courage to change. It requires the courage to break through all your current ideologies and conventions and all the barriers surrounding that. All this requires having a clear stance and a willingness to act upon it, which is what will shape the future. Without this courage for change, today and tomorrow will be exactly the same as yesterday.

Everything in this universe and in life exists in language. Everything you see and hear, smell, taste and touch have a language around it. Nothing exists without language. All of creation started with language. Before anything happens, you have a thought, this thought is described in words, and without those words you would not even know you are having a thought.

Everything we see in our environment whether it be the house we live in, the cars on the road, businesses or places we visit started with a thought, it is the people who expanded those thoughts that created what we see around us today, those thoughts started in language. It is the language around our thoughts that create the life we are currently living. It is those little words or context sentences that have the power to influence our subconscious mind in a positive or negative way.

"The Art of Language" is not about a new self-help technique, it is about expanding on what you already know. There are many books, coaches, teachers and motivational speakers in the world who all offer something special, bringing their unique experiences of self-development to help millions of people achieve their goals and dreams.

There are no wrong self-help techniques; they are all perfect in their unique nature and presentation. You may have learnt some or even many of these techniques, some have worked for you and some have not. This does not mean that those techniques that have not worked for you, don't work.

You are a unique individual and are special in many ways; therefore there are a number of reasons why some techniques may not have worked for you. In most cases the main reason why most of the techniques are not working for you, if tracked carefully, you will come to realise that it is due to the conversations or self-talk that has caused an unconscious resistance to achieving what you really want. This brings us back to the first point I made, everything is created in language.

"The Art of Language" is exactly that; an art, a skill which you have to develop. It is about looking at what you have already learnt in self-development and what is currently causing the obstacles and blocks that are preventing you from moving forward. It is about going back to the beginning of the whole process of the technique you have already learnt and identifying the language around that.

Once you are able to see how the language is affecting you subconsciously, you can then change the language around your goals and dreams that resonate with your subconscious mind which will help you overcome those obstacles and blocks. It is not going to be easy to constantly be aware of your language. You have been influenced and programmed to be the way you are for many years.

This subconscious influence and programming has created the behaviours and habits you have today. Therefore it is going to take some time as your subconscious mind will need some time to accept the new programming. You cannot just delete from your subconscious what is already there; it has to be replaced gradually.

This skill requires patience, dedication and persistence on your part. Once you are able to change the subconscious language and identify the words that powerfully resonates with your subconscious mind, you will be able to powerfully transform your life into the life you really want. All habits and behaviours are learnt from the time we are born, the good news is that what is learned can be un-learned, which means that all behaviours and habits can be modified to reduce the unconscious resistance that blocks us from achieving our dreams.

With practice it really does get easier as you move forward. You are not expected to get it right first time around, so do not put that expectation on yourself as so many people do. It took more than five years just to put all the material together for this book, therefore nobody expects you to get it one hundred percent right either.

Introduction

Some people may not even grasp some of the concepts the first time around, which is okay. There is no right or wrong here, just a willingness on your part to develop the skill around the words and language you use to create the life you want. The trick is to approach these techniques with no expectations but with a willingness to be in action to achieve your dreams.

It is not about getting it one hundred percent right or about having great results all the time but about transforming the words you use to expand on what you have already learnt to create the life you truly want without expectations. Expectations usually end up in disappointments; the focus is on transforming yourself internally to create the life you want externally.

All human beings have the right answers within themselves for what is possible to transform, all they need is to be guided to seeing those answers rather than giving them the answers directly. When answers are provided especially when it comes to self-development, human beings resist them. Therefore this book is written in a way that does not provide you with all the answers but leads you to that place of choice.

When you realise you have power of choice, you will automatically recognise the right answers for what is important to you. You will find that some of the chapters are open ended because you have the answers and only need to be guided to identifying them through your own power of choice. It is a journey and the best way to experience that journey is to have fun doing it. During this transformation process you will come to realise just how amazing, powerful, creative and special you really are.

Chapter 1
The Essence of You

I want you to take a minute here and put aside in this moment, everything you know, believe or perceive of the world. Put aside what you believe to be right or wrong, everything you know whether it is cultural, spiritual, religious or how things should be or work in this world. Even if some of you think that this is going esoteric, I encourage you to put aside all judgements and opinions in this moment.

Try and get to a place where your mind is clear and empty, try and avoid analysing this and just focus on getting your mind clear and empty. From this moment while your mind is in this empty space, I encourage you to open your mind to looking at a new way of creation.

This concept may be difficult to grasp at first, it might leave you feeling a little confused, there is no right or wrong to this. The aim here is to get you to really clear your mind for the purpose of opening yourself up to a powerful way to re-create your language of transformation.

Everything in the universe, in life or the whole of creation as we know it today was created in language. Without language nothing exists, there would be no memory of any existence. Your thought is based in language no matter what your mother tongue may be; whether it is English, French, German, Zulu or something else.

Without words or context sentences to describe that thought, you would not even know you are having a thought. You would not have memory of anything regarding your own existence if it was not for language to create and describe it. It is within this language, the words and context sentences that you speak to yourself in every moment that unconsciously affect your outcomes in life.

From the time we are in our mother's womb we are being programmed with language, whether it is the language of sound or emotion, this language affects us on the subconscious level and plays a role in the development of our future habits and behaviours. For example; when a baby is born, you will notice that the way the baby cries, its cry mimics the accent in which the mother speaks with.

If the mother of the new born baby speaks with a soft voice or tone, usually the baby cries with a soft tone. The opposite will happen if the mother has a loud voice or tone. As the baby grows it generally mimics the mother's habits and responds to mother's words. In many cases from the age of two, the child will start to either mimic the father's accent or the accent of its immediate social environment.

Up until the age of eight, we are living at the subconscious level; our conscious mind is only formed at eight years of age. This is when logic and reasoning start to play a role in our thinking. Before the age of eight, while living in the subconscious level, there is a lot of programing of our future habits, traits and behaviours. Between the age of eight and fourteen, while the conscious mind is being fully formed as well as our core traits, behaviours and the way we perceive the world is formed. It is also during this time where our behaviours towards future relationships start to form.

It is during this time part of our identity and traits such as whether we are extrovert or introvert are formed. The way we respond to suggestions or take in information is also formed during this stage of our lives. All of this started in some form of language and moulded the way we think today.

It is in this language of creation where we can modify behaviours at a subconscious level to improve our chances of creating a better life. Once the subconscious mind has been programmed with behaviours and habits, it becomes difficult to change those habits, thus the statement that it takes twenty one days to form a new habit.

Habits and Behaviours

Habits and behaviours can be modified at a subconscious level for positive transformation by gradually replacing old habits and behaviours over thirty to ninety days. You cannot just delete a habit or behaviour from your subconscious mind; it has to be replaced gradually.

The reason why most people struggle to make changes in their lives is due to this subconscious programming, when change starts to occur, even if it is positive change, the subconscious mind will resist, causing us to either fail at taking action or finding distractions that move us away from achieving our goals.

The simple reason for this is that what currently exists on the subconscious mind is a known. This is what puts us into automatic mode when it comes to behaviours and habits.

When you try to change the behaviour or habit, the new suggestion of the new behaviour or habit is an unknown to the subconscious mind even if it is positive and good for us, causing the subconscious mind to resist this new habit or behaviour. Any new habits or behaviours have to be programed one step at a time over thirty to ninety days.

Unless you know how to access your theta level of your subconscious mind, where a habit or behaviour can be replaced almost immediately, the next best form of quick habit and behaviour change is in language, the words and context sentences you use in your self-talk. Even these words and context sentences need to be practiced to give your subconscious mind some time to catch up and accept the new suggestion for transformation.

The subconscious mind makes up around ninety percent of your total mind, and it is the most powerful attribute of all human life. We have very little or no control over this level of mind. The subconscious mind has three levels, Alpha, theta and delta. Delta is the area we go into when we fall into deep sleep.

During this deep sleep your subconscious is usually active but we are never aware of it. Theta is the level just before deep sleep, that drowsiness you feel just before you fall asleep is the theta level. Alpha level is usually accessed when our bodies are completely relaxed. The conscious mind, which makes up ten percent of the mind, is the beta and gamma level, the level you are constantly in when fully awake.

The gamma level is usually accessed when the brain is highly stimulated from too much coffee or alcohol, some people reach high levels of gamma causing them to lose consciousness and any memory of being in that state. Between the conscious and subconscious mind lies the filter area which filters all the information we take in through our five senses throughout the day.

Our conscious mind cannot handle these thousands of information units coming in every second, it is the filter area that takes it in and only allows the most important things that we are dealing with in a given moment to be processed by the conscious mind. For example; when you are in conversation with someone, your conscious mind is only processing their face through sight, their voice and what is being said through hearing.

During this time you are not fully aware of what is going on around you. You are not aware of the shoes on your feet until someone brings it to your attention, at the same time you are not fully aware of all the other sounds around you even if you are hearing them. The filter area then only lets the information which is a known pass through to your subconscious mind and then releases all the unnecessary information during the REM sleep stage.

While the filter area is active, we remain in the beta state which makes it difficult to create new habits or break old ones. As mentioned earlier, the best and fastest way to create positive transformation is being able to access our theta level of mind. This is not always easy and most of the time most people will fall into deep sleep at this level.

The next best thing is language as language is the start of all creation. It is for this reason that at the beginning of this chapter, I asked you to put aside everything that you know or perceive to be right or wrong, judgements and opinions, beliefs and practices.

Put it aside in this moment as you open your mind to looking at creation in a new context. The purpose of this is to get your mind to a blank space so when you create the new language it is created from nothing; it is from this space of nothing where the subconscious mind will accept the new language faster than when practiced at the beta or conscious mind level.

In truth meditation and self-hypnosis would probably be the fastest way to creating this new language on the theta level of subconscious where transformation will begin almost immediately. We can access our alpha level of the subconscious mind quite easily, and I recommend you do this when clearing your mind to that empty space. It will also give you the opportunity to create the new language around your goals at this level, making it more powerful to motivate you into achieving that goal.

Accessing your Alpha

To access your alpha level of subconscious mind is so simple. All you have to do is sit in a comfortable chair keeping your back up straight. Start to breathe slowly and deeply in and out of your nose. Concentrate on this breathing until you start to feel relaxed. Once you start feeling relaxed, close your eyes gently and go back to concentrating on those slow deep breaths.

At this point you should be feeling fairly relaxed. You can imagine that your body is now relaxed from head to toe. Once you feel completely relaxed, you are in your alpha level. While you are sitting in your chair completely relaxed with your eyes closed, allow your mind to drift a little, just let your thoughts that are currently running through your mind to just flow no matter what those thoughts are.

After a minute or so, there is no specific time here, say the word STOP as sternly as you can. It does not matter whether you say STOP quietly in your mind or out loud, as long as you say it as sternly as possible. This should stop all those thoughts from flowing, if it does not work the first time round, don't let that bother you, it may take a few times of saying STOP before your mind begins to quiet down.

As you notice your mind quieting down, say the words in your mind "I command all thoughts to stop completely". You may have to repeat this a few times. If this is the first time you are trying this, it might take some time to get your mind to that quiet place. Do not let this discourage you, this is about your transformation so don't give your power up to those unnecessary thoughts going on inside your head.

If after ten minutes you find that your mind is still not quieting down, don't be hard on yourself, acknowledge yourself for trying and then open your eyes and go about your day. When you find time again either the same day or the next day, try and get to that relaxed state, the alpha level then state "I command all thoughts to STOP". After that keep repeating "All thoughts are now quieting down".

Believe in yourself, even if it takes more than three or four days to get to that quiet place of mind, you can do it, anyone can do it. Those who meditate can go into their meditation and access that completely still state of mind. Once you find you are getting to that quiet still state, you can move on to the next level.

Sit in this quiet still space for a few minutes; just be with that quietness and peace. After a few minutes try and imagine that everything in life comes from the same energy. This may sound esoteric or new age to some, it may even sound as if it goes against your conventions or beliefs, the aim here is not to teach you a new spirituality or belief, it is about getting your mind to a quiet place where you can learn to start creating a new language for your own creation of the life you want, it is about becoming one with your creativity and inner depths of your own subconscious mind.

Once you are able to get to that place where you can imagine that everything in life, be it the universe, planets, plants, animals and human beings are created from the same energy, some of you might need some time to grasp this, try and be in that energy of oneness. To help you better understand this; imagine a tank containing ten thousand litres of water. I give you ten thousand one litre bottles, each bottle has a different design on them, and no two bottles are the same. Now I ask you to fill each bottle with water from the ten thousand litre tank. Once you have filled each bottle, I ask you if the water in bottle number fifty is different to the water in bottles five thousand or nine thousand.

Chances are you will tell me "No" all the water in each bottle is the same because it all came from the same tank. In the same way, try to imagine that everything in life, no matter what it is, was created from the same place or energy. There is a connection to everything that exists including you, that same energy is contained within you and is connected to everything else that exists.

Once again I repeat that the important thing to remember is that this is about connecting to your creative self and becoming one with this energy that exists within you. Thought is energy and that energy is the same energy that exists within your body and mind.

The purpose of this whole exercise is to get you to a place in your mind where nothing exists, and from this non-existence there lies the possibility of creating something from nothing. When there is nothing then anything becomes possible to create.

You have been programmed for many years with a language that has to some extent brought some form of negative outcomes in your life. Creating a new language that will be accepted by your subconscious mind needs to be created with a new foundation and that is from a place of nothing or non-existence.

Once you are able to grasp that everything in life is connected and comes from the same energy, that same energy is thought and you are able to get your mind to a quiet place where you can imagine that nothing exists, from this point try and open your mind to a new way of looking at how creation occurred.

You don't have to believe in this at a conscious level, however the aim is to get your subconscious mind to accept the new language or whatever it is that you want to create for yourself without doubt. Sometimes the slightest doubt, even an atom's worth of doubt can become an obstacle in you achieving a goal. Doubt is so powerful it can negatively influence us into moving away from believing in ourselves or our ability to achieve much more than what we perceive to be possible.

Being able to get to that point in our mind where nothing exists, as well as looking at a different way of how creation occurs will eliminate that doubt and get you deeply connected with your creativity. Being one with your creativity allows you to experience your own inner essence in a more powerful way, the real essence of you.

Imagine for a moment that nothing exists, even the universe, absolutely nothing exists only pure energy. This pure energy is in constant motion as there is no time and space. Imagine as this timeless energy flows it is complete unity, it is the unlimited and it only exists in absolute oneness.

From this absolute unlimited oneness it transcends into self-essence, the thought or energy of thought, language begins at this point. This becomes power and light. From this self-essence, power and light, this energy transcends into knowledge and within this knowledge comes existence.

Within this awareness of existence the knowledge transcends into the energy of ultimate light, this could also be called spirit as it is energy form, do not confuse this spirit with spiritual or religious descriptions of it, try and stay within the context of what is being described here.

From this ultimate light; similitudes, that which is similar to all things that exist is created. Also within this ultimate light attributes are created, attributes of you and all creation, that which is unique to you and unique to all individual things. When these similitudes and attributes combine into one, the physical form or the body is created.

It is within this body we exist, created in the exact same way as all other physical form. This is the essence of you in all creation. Try and see yourself and all creation in this way while in the deep relaxed state of your clear mind. Keep your judgements and opinions clear from seeing creation in this way. Just allow yourself in this space to experience creation in this way and be within this context that this is the essence of you.

You may not be grasping this at this moment; there is no right or wrong here. This will take some time for you to be able to fully grasp this concept. You don't have to believe in this at a conscious level, the aim is to get you to a place in your subconscious level where you can create your positive language for transformation with little or no doubt and resistance.

There is an important reason for looking at creation or the essence of you in this way besides the aim of creating your own new language. Since the day you were born, you have constantly been influenced unconsciously by your family unit and social environment, which has largely programmed you to being who you are today.

This means that your current identity of who you really are is based on what others think you should be. If you look deeply within yourself you will come to realize that you live your life according to what others think and say about you and not who you declare yourself to be.

This will not only help you create your new power language but help you get in touch with who you really are and see the true identity of the powerful you that you truly meant to be. Once you are able to identify your own true identity of how you choose to see yourself and be in this world, you will find it easier not only to create your new powerful language but to achieve much more than what you think to be truly possible. You will express yourself in a whole new way with an attitude of really being successful.

Now we can put all of this into perspective that will help you gain an understanding of this concept. When you are feeling relaxed with your mind clear, in an empty space. You imagine that nothing exists; only pure energy; this pure energy is the unity, the unlimited, the absolute oneness.

Imagine that you are this energy in that unity, unlimited and absolute oneness. Allow yourself to feel this if you can. You transcend into your essence where the light is your thought. In this place where you start to feel your essence, you have choice. In this choice you can choose to experience unconditional love. This is not the love that you feel for your parents, family, partners or friends; it is an unconditional love for yourself.

You may not feel it at first but with practice you can imagine this unconditional love flowing into your heart. Within this space of choice; you can now also choose happiness. This is the real love and happiness with which you have the option to choose. The purpose of choosing this love and happiness in this moment is to break the ego when you start to create the language for your positive transformation.

You have probably heard many coaches, teachers and motivational speakers saying that money or things don't make you happy, finding that special person does not make you happy. You can be happy with someone but they don't create your happiness, you do. Happiness is a choice and learning to first be happy before achieving your goals, brings the best results.

When you are able to feel this unconditional love and happiness in that quiet space of your mind, allowing it to flow to your heart, you can create the things you want in your life with love and passion. When you create from this space of love and passion and not your ego, you create for you with the ability to share with others. In this new life of creation, you don't need to create for status, admiration or fame and glory, but purely creating for yourself for the pure joy of it.

Within this space of unconditional love for self; a true deep self-love, there is more acceptance of your current situation without judgement or having to compare yourself to others. Through your acceptance of the current situation no matter what it may be, you are able to find your own true happiness.

In this moment there is less judging, comparing and focusing on what is wrong, there is just acceptance of it and in this calm place you will find solutions to getting out of those situations. Once you feel that unconditional love and happiness, you start to experience your own true power. From here you are able to transcend to a space of knowing, knowledge and existence.

You start to feel your true existence and within this knowledge you create the language of what you want. The language of what you want is the ultimate light, the similitudes and attributes of what you choose to bring into your life. There is no expectations in this moment therefore there are no disappointments.

In this space you become aware of opportunities and are able to take action to achieve your goals with love and joy for yourself which brings it into your life in physical form. In this moment you are not chasing what you want but attracting it to you through the path of least resistance.

The aim is to create a language through words and context sentences that honour you in the essence of you, while creating a powerful acceptance in your subconscious mind that you truly deserve to have the best that you can have. This is also a form of training your mind to have it now, creating the ability to achieve what you want with very little resistance in taking action on the goals you want to achieve. When you train your mind first the body will follow.

If you still have not grasped this concept yet, there is nothing wrong with that, go easy on yourself and don't worry about it. The important thing to understand is that you have the choice of being happy no matter what the circumstances may be right now. When choosing to feel that deep unconditional self-love, you become more accepting of whom you are. It is in this acceptance where the real change begins.

You start to feel true happiness and through this self-love, happiness and acceptance you are able to accept your circumstances and realise that it is only temporary. You start to feel your true power and realise that you have the ability to powerfully change your circumstances.

You will learn a new language that will put your current circumstances and issues into a new context that will help you resolve difficult situations, overcome obstacles and solve problems with little resistance and ease. You get to powerfully choose what you want in your life for the pure joy of it rather than chasing it for the purposes of the ego of success, status and fame.

It is in this space where you will come to realise that when you transform yourself internally, the universe and everything around you will adapt to your transformation without you having to fix or transform anything or anyone else around you. You will start to feel the true power within you, having the ability to achieve what you want with love and passion, experiencing the true essence of you in a powerful context.

Chapter 2
The Impact of "NO"

There are two little letters, the letter "N" and the letter "O" which put together spell the little word "NO" that impacts your life in more ways than you can even imagine. There is a very strong unconscious emotional attachment to this little word that most people don't even realise it exists.

This strong emotional attachment keeps you stuck in events of the past without you even being able to recognise it. The impact of this is that this unconscious emotional attachment to this little word prohibits you from moving forward in life or achieving more than what you believe to be possible. It is like a huge invisible wall blocking you in transforming or being in action in most areas of your life.

It may seem like a petty or little thing to be impacted by this little word in such a huge way; the reality is that it affects you in a number of ways. The emotional attachment is at an unconscious level and it is for this reason you are unable to recognize exactly how this little word impacts you. The subconscious impact of this little word "NO" affects people in different stages of their life.

Some are impacted by this word during their childhood, others during the teenage years and some in their twenties. It does not matter when this unconscious impact or emotional attachment began; it has the same negative impact or outcome with almost everyone. This negative impact can remain with you throughout your life.

Jenni's Story

Imagine the following scenario for a moment, think back to your childhood and try to identify if you can relate to the story.

Young Jenni who is in the 8th grade, walks past Ms Smith's class and notices that Ms Smith is alone in the class. Jenni walks into the classroom and greets Ms Smith. Jenni asks Ms Smith if she could help her with a project. Ms Smith says "No" because she has to leave but maybe she could help tomorrow. The moment Jenni heard the word "No", she filtered out the last part of the sentence "maybe tomorrow".

In that moment Jenni decides that Ms Smith does not like her and is not willing to help her. The result of this is that Jenni will always avoid or never ask Ms Smith for help again because she now believes that Ms Smith will always say "No". This does not end there, when Jenni decided that Ms Smith does not like her, Jenni starts to think "I am not good enough".

This impacts Jenni in many ways because she now has created a distance in relationships between her and teachers. From that moment on, Jenni struggles to ask any teacher for help. That one little "No" has caused Jenni to unconsciously create an emotional attachment to it, causing Jenni to struggle to ask for help even into adulthood.

At the same time Jenni unconsciously created that emotional attachment to the word "No", she had also decided that Ms Smith does not like her or that she is not good enough. This causes Jenni to feel insecure, constantly questioning whether teachers, people of authority or even peers, like her or not. The impact of this one little event has created insecurity in Jenni's life where she is afraid to ask for help, causing her to procrastinate on starting or completing projects, getting things done where she needs to ask for help.

Jenni's unconscious emotional attachment to that word "No" blocks Jenni from being able to see herself as bigger than she really is, even blocking her from achieving her true potential throughout her life. This does not necessarily mean that Jenni will not achieve success or great things in her life, on the contrary, two scenarios will occur for Jenni. She will either grow up struggling to ask for help and getting things done, leading to a mediocre life with a dead end job or she will be a high achiever.

Most people like Jenni will end up struggling through life, either just getting by or stuck in a job that does not bring much fulfilment. On the other hand, there will be people like Jenni that will achieve financial success and even do some great things in life, the difference being that they will do it all by themselves, causing other areas of their life to be neglected, areas such as relationships with others and even living a completely introvert life with not much social activity. This will differ from person to person depending on their core traits and personality. These scenarios of life all occurred because of that one little word "No".

Think back to the time when you were in school. Remember when you put your hand up to answer a question that the teacher asked, instead of calling on you, she called on someone else. Most people in that moment decide that the teacher does not like them or that they are not good enough.

Maybe the teacher did call on you and you got the answer wrong; most of your fellow pupils laughed. Most people in that moment of feeling embarrassed decide that they are not good enough. What do you think went through your mind in that moment? The reality is that most people never put their hand up again to answer questions whether it is in a class, seminar or meeting for the rest of their life; unless they are absolutely sure they know the topic or answer.

A lot of people develop the fear of getting it wrong or being laughed at so they just sit quietly even if they know the answer. The other impact this has on most people is that they become afraid to ask questions. These people will sit quietly and not put up their hand to ask questions if they don't understand what is being taught or said in the class, seminar or meeting. They just try and understand the best they can, afraid to put up their hand to ask questions because they fear that their question may not be good enough or even laughed at. Can you relate to this or even the scenario of Jenni's story?

You may be wondering right now, what does putting up your hand to ask or answer questions have to do with the impact of the word "No"? Both create another fear that starts to creep up during those early years of development and that is the fear of rejection. This usually happens at an unconscious level which most people are not even aware of.

However this is not always the same outcome with everyone, some people don't develop that fear of rejection until they actually experience some form of direct rejection. The impact or emotional attachment to the word "No" can leave one feeling rejected even if it is something simple like asking to borrow a pen.

In the same way when you put your hand up to answer the teacher's question, the teacher did not call upon you leaving you feeling like the teacher does not like you, it can be experienced as a form of rejection. The reality is that these are small events that happened in the past, it is the emotional attachment to these past experiences that makes the issue feel bigger than what it really is.

When faced with the situation in the present time of having to put your hand up to ask or answer a question, ask for help or even making requests, the subconscious mind triggers those negative emotions caused during those past events, causing you to either back off or struggle to ask for what you need with confidence. It is that emotion attached to those past events that are the biggest blocks to moving forward in certain or specific areas of your life.

The emotional attachment to that little word "No" can have another effect on you and that is the inability to say "No". Most people struggle to say "No" at the best of times. One of the main reasons for this is that the word "No" becomes associated with rejection on the subconscious level.

When you are confronted with a request, you know you cannot manage to fulfil that request, you know that you must say "No" but you just cannot say it, you feel butterflies in your stomach and emotional sensations throughout your body, causing you to reluctantly say yes. This has a spiralling effect on some people; they take on extra work, knowing that they will struggle to manage, causing them to fail at meeting deadlines in some areas and so on.

With some people they just cannot say "No" when someone is trying to sell them something and they end up buying things they don't need. Can you relate to this? Can you relate to the times when you knew you should have said "No" but grudgingly said"Yes"? In the end it caused you to have some sort of resentment towards the other person. The resentment sometimes leads to anger and hatred, the negative emotions just keep spiralling on and on with no end in sight.

All of this caused by one little incident where you were told "No" when you asked for something or for help. Every time somebody says "No" to you or when you have to say "No" to someone, you get those body sensations and the only time you are able to say "No" to something is when you finally get angry.

That anger then causes a rift with you and the person you have to say "No" to. This leaves some people having a lack in confidence, feeling insecure and having difficulty when trying to move forward in life. The subconscious will always trigger those emotions when the word "No" has to be used in certain situations, either making requests, asking for help or even saying "No" to a request or sales person.

This does not end there; some people get into the habit of saying "No" through little lies and excuses. Every time they are asked to do something or go somewhere by a particular person they will think up some excuse of why they cannot do it and so on rather than just saying "No".

The end result is that the lies will always have to be covered up with more lies until eventually they get caught out because they cannot remember what they said in the first place. This is a vicious circle that is not productive in any way. There are also people who have great ideas and the potential to start and run successful businesses, however when they get one or two "No's" either for financing or backing for their ideas, they simply give up, creating stories that there are no opportunities for people like them.

Then there are those who constantly complain of their situation or jobs, when they are given good ideas on how to improve themselves, they find all the excuses in the book to justify why they can't do it. It is just a story they keep telling themselves to get out of taking responsibility for themselves, it's just so easy to always blame someone else and to keep being the victim.

Nobody ever gets very far with that victim attitude, they always find themselves following the herd or in herd mentality as I like to call it. The list seems to have no end, there is always another story to tell or add to those negative emotional attachments. The question is; does the emotional attachment to that little word "No" attract more "No's" over and over again?

It is possible, especially on the subconscious level, the subconscious always triggers those emotions and human beings usually attract more negative situations when their emotions are negative. Think about it; how many times have you been faced with a situation where you had to go ask for something and you start making up stories in your head, "What if they say no" or "I know they are going to say no" and the what if just keeps going on in your head. In that moment you had already decided for the other person, you decided "No" for them so what do you get? Chances are you will keep getting that "No".

There is a simple solution to all of this. Remember that the "No" you got told or the rejection you may be feeling, all occurred in the past. You cannot physically get up from where you are to go into your actual past; therefore the past does not exist. Your past only exists in your present as memory or emotional attachment. This memory can be visual, verbal or in deep feelings in certain parts of your body.

It does not matter in what form your memory exists, all memory and emotional attachment's core existence is in the language created around it. Usually the language around the memory is exaggerated, making the situation feel bigger than what it really is; usually the emotional attachment is centred on the exaggerated language of the memory.

This language is like verbally beating yourself up, or a verbal self-sabotage. Think back to some of the times where you got told "No" or felt some form of rejection, whether it be in a classroom, a seminar, at work or at home, what were the words that went through your head in that moment?

Most people start saying to themselves, "I'm not good enough" or "he or she does not like me". Some people even use a little more harsh statements like "I don't belong here", "He or she is just being nasty to me" or "I'm stupid" and so on. These little negative words actually exaggerate the situation, making it more negative than it really is. The simple solution is to change the words. It is the first step to breaking that emotional attachment that is such a huge block that prevents you from moving forward.

Think back to all the times you were told "NO" especially the times when you felt rejected and unwanted. I'm not talking about intimate relationships at this point. Try and get in touch with those emotions around the "No" that you can remember. The stronger the emotion, chances are that the language around that incident was either harsh or ended up as a full blown story.

You don't have to remember the exact words you thought at the time, just be in tune with the emotion. Remember there is a story around these incidences and chances are the older you got the story gets longer. The reality is that the impact starts between the age of eight and mid-teens, however there are some people whose impact may have started at five years of age and some as late as eighteen or nineteen.

When we get to our twenties, we are not impacted directly by the word "No" but triggered by the past memory or unconscious emotional attachment to the "No" or feeling of rejection of the past. Think back to each of the incidences you can remember and state to yourself; "The 'No' that I was told in that moment was not a 'No' directed at me personally but to the request of that moment".

The truth is that you in that very moment made that 'No' mean something about you, this does not make you wrong in any way; it was what you knew at the time. The 'No' was nothing more than the person not being able to fulfil on the request in that moment. You may need to repeat the statement a number of times before the emotion starts fading away. Once you stop making the 'No' about you, there will be a break in the emotional attachment, setting you free from the burden of not being able to move forward, ask for help or make requests with confidence.

When it comes to intimate relationships, the dynamics are very different and it will differ from each couple's situation. Generally it all boils down to a breakdown in communication and the self-talk going on in each individual's head. Generally most people are talking at each other or past each other seldom hearing what is actually being said and thus causing conflict.

Generally once you have decided on how you perceive the other person to be, you only listen to them with that one perspective which leads to conflict. However there are more reasons for conflict and sometimes there are extreme cases and some of them may lead to emotional or even physical abuse.

This cannot be resolved by just changing the language or self-talk, it cannot be solved in one paragraph or chapter. In such cases it is best to seek the advice or help of licenced relationship councillors. The purpose of this book deals specifically with the self-talk that prohibits individuals from being in action or lacking in the ability to achieve their goals, it is to enhance what you already know in terms of self-development through changing your internal language when you come up against obstacles.

Therefore the self-talk discussed here when it comes to intimate relationships is a more general approach based on generalised issues that individuals may be dealing with, it is about changing your internal representation of self to help you recognise that you have the power to resolve situations even if it may require requesting help.

The reality is that when individuals are dealing with issues of low self-esteem, finances, feeling powerless, anger or bitterness towards others or at work, they tend to take it out on the person closest to them. It is a way of feeling some form of power. Usually the self-talk is exaggerated around the feeling or words of not being good enough, feeling useless or unworthy and in most cases a self-hatred.

When there is some form of rejection in these relationships, the general tendency is self-talk of not feeling worthy, unwanted, powerless, inadequate and even making oneself wrong. The first step is to keep reminding yourself that you are worthy, deserving of better and don't have to submit to being wrong all the time.

This is not about making the other person right or wrong or even making you right. It is about changing that self-talk that leaves you feeling powerless to that which will help you start realising that you have the power to change your situation. It is the past 'No's' or rejections that are triggered in those moments of rejection in intimate relationships that exaggerate the story or internal talk of not being good enough or unworthy.

As you will learn in the following chapters it really is all about changing that self-hatred into self-love which is done through changing the words or context sentences of your self-talk.

Other than the dynamics mentioned in intimate relationships, the important thing to remember is not to make the 'No' about you personally. It is what happened in the moment whether the teacher did not call on you or you got the answer wrong; that is all it is nothing more. When people told you 'No' it was not about you but them being unable to help you or fulfil on the request in that moment.

Even if there may be conflict between you and the other person or maybe you know that the other person does not like you, even in those circumstances it helps to change the context in your language. Changing the context means allowing yourself to not take the 'No' or rejection personally but stating that it is what it is in that moment.

Keeping the statements short and simple is the key to getting the context changed as the subconscious mind responds best to simplicity. The purpose of this is to avoid getting into that space of anger and self-hatred. It is in this new context where you can start creating a new language for positive transformation.

Another way of overcoming the impact of 'No' is by practicing to say 'No' or receiving a 'No'. One way of doing this is getting a friend or a partner to assist you. Tell them to offer you things and even if it is things that you want, keep saying 'No' until you feel the emotion fade completely. Then instruct the friend or partner to keep saying 'No' to your requests for this exercise.

Ask them for things or make requests allowing them to say 'No' until the emotion fades completely. Once you have broken through these emotional barriers of the impact of 'No' you will start to live your life in a whole new context. You will find it easier to be persistent at achieving what you want no matter how many 'No's' you might get along the way. You will stop thinking of the "What if they say No" and just go ahead and make your requests without expectations. Remember this is something that takes time to overcome and with practice you will get it right, allowing you to move forward on your path to positive transformation.

Chapter 3
The Effects of Words

There are moments when the words of others can affect us in so many ways without us even realising it. It is these subtle moments when we least expect it, a word or statement gets drawn in at a deep unconscious level that it affects us throughout our lives or until we become aware of it.

I am not talking about hurtful words that people may say when you are in direct conversation or in an argument with them. I am not even referring to the times when you may be receiving some criticism for something or took offence to a joke that was made, this also includes the times when someone or people in your family are saying things in anger towards you.

Although during these times those words do hurt, most people get over them fairly quickly and they do not affect you on a deep unconscious level throughout your life. I am referring to times when you may have been sitting quietly reading or just relaxing, even just having a quiet moment or quietly busy in the middle of something, when someone comes and says something innocently in passing, usually this is one little statement or sentence.

These subtle moments when one word in that statement could become a deep unconscious cause of the way you look at yourself for the rest of your life. These subtle moments usually occur during our childhood or teenage years, and are usually the words or statements of our siblings or parents as they make a statement in passing.

Remember the statements made in passing were done so innocently therefore there is no blame here. In that moment you were unware that one little word was going to impact you for the rest of your life. Generally we do become aware of these impact words and are able to overcome them with proper self-development or in this case recreating the language of that moment on the subconscious level.

One way that most women are affected by this passing statement throughout their lives is in the area of their weight. Between the ages of eight and fourteen, a sibling, parent or guardian may have said in passing, "You look fat in that".

In that subtle moment your subconscious mind may have been fully open, either because your body was completely relaxed or you were deep in thought while in the middle of something. In that moment the word 'fat' unconsciously impacted you and from that moment onwards you decided that you were fat.

This becomes a lifelong issue, usually covered up in statements like "It is in my generic makeup" or "I comfort eat because of emotional situations" and so forth. No matter what the symptoms or reasons of your weight issue, it all boils down to that one unconscious moment when the word impacted you.

One thing to remember though is that this may not always be the case, there could be some health issues that could be causing weight problems. Unhealthy eating due to lifestyle could be another cause. There could have been an unconscious programing before the age of eight where most of the people in your family could be dealing with weight issues and this could become an unconscious programing that only starts to affect you much later in life.

There are a whole lot of other reasons for the cause of weight issues. However most of the time these issues lie in the language or self-talk which exaggerates the situation causing people to become what they feel. Usually it is within that emotional attachment that was created in the decision of "I am fat" that makes it so difficult to break through that feeling and work toward creating the new language of transformation to achieve what you want.

I am not suggesting here that by just changing your language around your weight issues that everything will transform magically into that ideal body you want. The truth is that it is not going to be so easy. You have had these issues for so long that you are programmed on a deep subconscious level into believing that you are the way you are.

It is this belief that is hardest to break through as well as creating a new self-belief that will be fully accepted by the subconscious mind. On the subconscious level, when you believe something without doubt, it becomes a known and in that known it shows up physically in your life.

It is due to this known or belief on the subconscious level that one would continuously be looking for ways to combat the weight issue either through excessive exercise, diets and so on. Some people even have the extreme attachment of feeling fat even if they are not. It is like a vicious cycle that keeps going on and on with no end in sight.

Changing that known belief into the new belief of what you want your body to be will not just work on affirmations or language but a whole new belief on the subconscious level through the new created language. Creating that new belief will take some time and will differ from person to person. During this time people will continue to be triggered with weight issues as the subconscious will resist.

The important thing is to accept the current situation for what it is, and then be persistent in getting the subconscious mind to accept the new language. As you will learn in the following chapters, creating the new language is the first step to transformation, and it is about using the new language around the steps you are already taking to resolve the issues that you may be dealing with currently.

There are many ways in which the words of others can impact us especially during our childhood. When siblings say on a regular basis that you are stupid or dumb because of something you did innocently, or maybe even made a mistake, this can influence your subconscious mind into believing that you are not good enough even if it may not be true.

Sometimes where there are two sisters and the one sister gets called beautiful by others and the other sister is told that she is pretty, the one who is told that she is pretty starts to believe that her sister is beautiful and she is not. Sometimes this causes her to become introvert and either be totally academically focused which causes her to neglect other areas of her life especially in creating healthy social circles. Otherwise she becomes an under achiever and tends to concentrate on activities where she will not be seen much.

There are more dynamics to this. However this is only a basic description of some of the causes of the effects of other people's words. Sometimes actions of others can be perceived into language that causes a child to believe they are not good enough. If a child perceives that the parent is giving the sibling more attention, this could cause the child to believe they are not good enough. This is created in the child's own internal self-talk.

Sibling rivalry can also be a contributing factor to the child deciding they are not good enough, especially when there are a lot of comparisons being made between the siblings by the parents or guardians. When parents start to compare their children to other people's children, for example when a parent says to his or her child "Look at how wonderful Mrs Smith's child is", this is usually said in anger by a parent when there is some sort of reprimand going on.

Usually in this moment the child decides "I am not good enough" which then impacts that child for the rest of their life. Even though some of those words may have been said in anger or frustration, and thereafter the parent calms down and says sorry and assures the child that they are still loved, there is a strong chance in that subtle moment when the words were drawn in at an unconscious level and the belief of not being good enough was created.

Sometimes a minor action by the parent in a given moment may be perceived by the child as abandonment, even if the event of that moment is forgotten within a few days. The abandonment feeling will start to show up in other areas of the child's life as the child moves into the teenage years.

Remember that these are descriptions of possible incidents of childhood that occurred in fairly stable homes. Where there are situations such as alcohol abuse by parents, causing the home environment to be difficult, where there is physical or sexual abuse in the home, the dynamics are completely different and one cannot just rely on the recreation of language to create the transformation, in such cases it is best for the individual to get professional help or work with a coach in order to get the best benefit for a positive outcome.

The recreation of language in this case could only possibly help the individual get to the realisation that they are powerful enough to request the help they need so that they can create the life they truly want. I truly believe that anything is possible even if some of the time it may seem unrealistic or unachievable. It does take a lot of courage to work on self-transformation. Self-transformation has never been easy, if it were, we would all be living the lives we wanted with very little effort.

There are some statements that are quite laughable but the funny thing is that they actually impact us in some way, causing us to have some belief of lack or limit. Have you ever heard the statement "You can't have your bread buttered on both sides"? Really! Have you ever taken a slice of bread and buttered it on both sides? You can do that and still eat it, it may be very messy but you can eat it.

The question is what does that statement mean? Who came up with that statement? In my view that statement was created from a limited mind set. The other famous statement "You can't have your cake and eat it", what does that really mean? Have you ever met anyone who has baked a cake and the moment it came out of the oven, they put it into a glass case for permanent display?

I know bakers put cakes in glass counters for the purpose of resale, however that statement of "You can't have your cake and eat it" really does not make sense and probably also created from a limited mind set. The reality is that these nonsensical statements can cause a mind-set of lack or limit, especially during the teenage years.

Another famous statement that causes the belief that one has to live with limits or lack is that statement "Money is the route of all evil". Since when did money get life that it became the route of all evil? Money is only a lifeless object that is used for the exchange of goods and services.

Have you ever had money jump out of your bank account, wallet or purse to go do some mischief or evil? It is only the nonsense in an individual's head that can be the route to all evil. I have met rich and poor people who have done something construed as evil. So how does money suddenly get life to become evil?

The sad reality is that those who believe that statement end up believing that it is better to have a lack or limited life, even to the extent that it is best to struggle through life. These are all little exaggerated self-talk going on in people's heads that disallow them from seeing their true potential.

When parents have conversations about money around their young children, especially if those conversations are about the lack of money or how difficult things are financially, chances are those words are going to affect the young child subconsciously later on in life.

This might not always be the case especially if that child grows up and ends up doing the job he or she loves. Generally though there will always be some negative conversations around money. Social environment especially in areas where there is a lot of poverty, can affect children on the subconscious level. Generally in these areas the conversation is around lack or not having.

There is no one to blame here, it is what it is in these areas. Most people who grow up in such circumstances really struggle to dream big, not because they can't but from an unconscious level they can't fully grasp what abundance really is. The sad reality is that most people who don't get the opportunity to have a tertiary education, believe that they are limited in what they can do, thus leading to a life of difficulty and struggle.

These people find it hard to understand on a mental level what having abundance really is, even if they are able to consciously dream of having an abundant lifestyle. There are many other factors that affect people in such cases however the impact is generally the same and therefore it is not necessary to get bogged down into each and every factor. The important thing to understand is that it is all in the unconscious language which becomes the exaggerated self-talk.

Other ways where people are affected by unconscious impacts are when people are afraid to do things because they are worried about what others will think. Have you ever sat with a group of people and suddenly you share a great idea that you have been pondering about for a while.

When you hear the responses generally most of the people in the group have already decided that your idea won't work. This decision is based on their own fears and feeling of lack. Nobody provides any proven facts of why your idea will not work, they just claim it does not work and will come up with whatever excuse is available to justify their claim.

Once this happens you decide that your idea is not good enough and abandon the idea altogether, an opportunity lost all because of what others said. Some people are afraid to share or act on their ideas because they think others will think it's stupid.

It's so amazing how people go into thinking for others mode. Then there are all the "What if's" and the "Yes but" and the list goes on and on. A lot of good ideas have been lost all because people decide that others may not like their idea or others have put their fears forward by justifying why ideas don't work.

The sad reality of all of this is that most people never get to experience their true potential and will never find out whether their wonderful ideas will work or not all because of other people's fears and justifications. Once again all of this boils down to the exaggerated language going on in the head about something that has not even become a reality yet.

What others think or say about you is none of your business. The reality is when you worry about what others are thinking or saying about you, all you are doing is taking ownership of their negativity. It is in this worry where you create a whole exaggerated self-talk that holds you back from following your own passion or achieving the things that you really want.

People who have achieved the greatest things are the ones who ignored what others said. Many great people in the past were called mad or bonkers yet they went on to achieve many great things all because they ignored what others said. When you take ownership of the negative words or thoughts of others, you are in reality creating a whole new negative language about yourself.

Even if you are absolutely certain that someone does not like you or if you know for sure that there are people gossiping about you, it is none of your business. The reality is that when people gossip, what they are really talking about is their own negativity or something that is missing in their own lives. It is much easier to cast blame than to take responsibility, people don't like the reality of having to deal with themselves.

They are triggered into gossiping about others because they fail to acknowledge or recognise their own flaws or negativity, so they have to find someone else to put down just so they can feel better about themselves. The next time you are triggered in a negative way by someone, ask yourself what is missing in your life that you were triggered in this negative way.

Avoid creating right and wrong here but merely ask the question. Don't try and think up an answer, ask the question in a calm manner and you will be surprised at the answers that will automatically come up. Those answers may not come up immediately but they eventually do come up. The aim here is to train you to start taking responsibility for your own life and being accountable for it, rather than taking the easy way out and playing the blame game, which never gets anyone anywhere.

There are thousands of ways that we could have been unconsciously impacted by the words or actions of others, some of them being subtle moments where things were said in innocence, family or social environments and many more, some cases more extreme than others.

The important thing to remember is that it is not absolutely necessary to identify exactly where and when or even each of the thousands of words that may have impacted you. Chances are that you will be wasting valuable time and not even know exactly where to start.

It will be like looking for something but you don't even know what you are looking for.

As you will learn in the following chapters; the trick is to identify the very first time you felt the negative emotion or thought, for example when was the very first time you felt fat? When was the very first time you began to think you were not good enough? From there you can try and identify what was the event that caused you to feel that way or decide that is who you are.

Once you have identified that, you can then start creating the new language on defining who you really are. The reality is that defining or creating the new language to define you is the easy part, the hard part is to break through all the negative emotions attached to those subtle moments that impacted you.

The aim here is not to get bogged down into all the different ways that you could have been impacted but to have a basic general understanding on how you could have been impacted or how the effects of words, whether it comes from others or yourself, can greatly influence your life.

It is within this context that causes you to run up against obstacles when trying to create a new life. The resistance to change all lies in the unconscious language already programmed onto the subconscious mind and the emotional attachments to those events. Changing your language is the easy part; it is having the courage to fight those resistance, attachments and negative emotions that will require some effort, as well as being consistent and persistent if you really want that positive transformation.

Chapter 4
Self-Talk

Self-talk is all those conversations going on in your head at any given time, cluttering your mind with a lot of unnecessary words that hold no value to you what so ever. It is the exaggerated stories that you created over time, based on one simple little event that occurred years ago.

These stories get so long that you probably could write a book about them. Chances are that over the years half of that exaggerated story is nothing more than nonsense and has no meaning or connotation to the original event or situation. These are all the stories that we start to make up about others and ourselves, how the world seems to be and everything else that could be wrong in it.

Usually these stories make the events or situations look much bigger than what it really was. These stories keep you stuck in the past and no matter how much you want positive transformation, some of these stories are so unconsciously rooted into your subconscious, they play a role in what your current behaviour and patterns are towards the way you live your life in each given moment.

In truth, you may think you living in the present; the reality is your habits are causing you to act out the past, which in turn shows up in your future. It is within this self-talk that you do the things you do, go about your daily tasks and get stuck in the repetition of each day happening over and over the same way every time. Today feels like yesterday and chances are that tomorrow will feel like today, all because you have had the same self-talk going on in your head the whole time.

The majority of the conversations going on within the self-talk are around self-doubt, self-limitations and most negative of them all, self-hatred. Most people don't realise the self-hatred they cause to themselves through the language they have created about themselves.

In most cases it does not even feel or seem to resemble self-hatred so it becomes difficult to recognize that it actually is self-hatred. Most people will go into denial about this because it is an area or topic that is so difficult to accept. The hardest job in life is the job of dealing with oneself. When it comes to dealing with self, most people are too afraid to deal with what is really there, it is much easier to resist, brush it under the carpet or blame circumstances than it is to take on responsibility.

Take a closer look and notice just how easy it is to play the victim rather than to rise above that because there is an unwillingness to accept and deal with the ugly bits of self. Most people would rather verbally beat themselves up than to see situations or events for what they really are. It is so much easier to create a victim story around an event or situation than it is to leave it for what it is.

For example; imagine you doing something in the kitchen and you suddenly turn to pick something up but in the process you knock over a glass and it rolls off the counter and smashes onto the floor. The event is that you knocked a glass over and it fell and broke. In most cases people start being harsh on themselves, saying things like "Oh you idiot, don't you watch what you're doing?", or maybe "I am so clumsy" and so on.

Rather than seeing the event for what it is, the glass fell and broke nothing else, people will create stories even as far as going to the "What if's" like "If only I was more careful" or "If only I had put the glass somewhere else" and so on. All of that self-talk is so irrelevant and has got nothing to do with the event.

When things like this happen, no matter how small or big the event, it is just so easy to create a negative story about self than it is to leave the event at what it really is. People do this in almost every aspect of their life, and it just continues on and on.

We are human and we are going to make mistakes, get distracted or just be in a deep thought from time to time, accidents will happen during these times, there is no need to beat oneself up about it. These may seem like little statements over a tiny or simple event, it is these little self-beating statements that are the seeds which grow the self-hatred.

Some people will suffer bigger events or trauma than others in their lifetime, while there will be those who generally have a fairly easy life, despite this and no matter what the cause of our circumstances, we all create that self-talk that spirals us into some sort of difficulty at some point in our life.

Within this self-talk there are emotional attachments to the situation or event that make the situation or event stay stuck in our minds. It is these emotional attachments that are the hardest to deal with and does take some courage to break through them. Over and above all of that, we are constantly comparing ourselves to others thinking that they are way better off than us.

When we get into this negative spiral, we start to believe that we are the only ones going through that specific situation and thus make the event or situation ten times bigger than what it really is. It is only when we start to realise that there are others who are going through similar situations of what we are experiencing can we then realise that the problem is smaller than what we think it really is.

Unfortunately the reality of life is that there are always going to be people who are better off or worse off than you. When you start comparing yourself to those who are better off than you, you create a language in your subconscious that makes you feel as if you are not good enough, slowly spiralling you into that self-hatred.

When it comes to those who are worse off than you, sometimes the tendency or ego makes you look down on them just so you can feel better about yourself. The truth is you are still creating a self-hate because that looking down is a negative and even though you tend to feel better about yourself, your subconscious mind is reading it as "I don't deserve better than this", causing you to struggle to really achieve the things you want.

The subconscious mind cannot distinguish between reality and fantasy; it always perceives what it sees as real. In the same way when you are talking negatively or looking down on another person or situation, the subconscious mind will always relate that back to you and associate it with one or more negative events or situations in your life.

What this really means is that when you are speaking negatively whether it is about a situation, circumstance or someone else, the subconscious mind reflects that conversation as being a part of you, even if the situation or circumstance has got nothing to do with you. The subconscious mind creates the impression in language that you are actually speaking about yourself and will trigger something similar to occur in your life or create negative emotions that will block you from moving forward in life.

I know that this might be a little confusing or even hard to grasp. This is not easy to grasp especially if you struggle to understand how it is possible that when you are speaking of something that really has got nothing to do with you; how does it become a part of you? The answer is simple; remember that everything in life is created in language, nothing can exist without this language, it is within this language that is going on in your head that the subconscious mind will associate it with you or as being your life.

It is for this reason why we never get exactly what we want no matter how much we strive for it. There is a constant conflict of language or self-talk going on inside our heads that causes chaos on the subconscious level that prevents us from creating the exact life that we constantly dream about.

We create high expectations and then we are disappointed because that expectation has not been met according to our standards or thoughts. No matter how much or how hard some people try, they just cannot seem to get to where they want to be. Although you may be in a positive state of mind when it comes to achieving your goal, the one thing that slows you down from getting there quickly is there probably is the unconscious feeling of "I am not good enough" or "I don't deserve this" going on which could have been created from a past experience or during your childhood.

This causes conflict with your subconscious mind as you are focused on what you want but there is doubt being caused because of that unconscious feeling of self. This could lead to either fear of success or fear of failure. Fear of success is when you are constantly worried whether you are going to be able to handle the success or whether you will be able to manage and maintain it.

The fear of failure is when you are constantly working many hours a day trying to keep your head above water so that you don't fail at anything causing you to neglect other areas of your life such as relationships or even health. There could be many factors that cause you to have these fears and doubts, the main reason and the most powerful reason of them all is the words or context sentences centred on them that exaggerate the feeling of doubt or fear.

Once you can identify the words or language being used that exaggerates the fear or doubt, you can start to change the language around that which will help break through those emotional barriers that keep you blocked. However it is important to remember that just changing the language is not going to make things suddenly happen magically, you have to keep practicing this new language for a month or two so that the subconscious mind can accept the new programming.

Self-doubt can be a major barrier in your life, much bigger than you can imagine. Even the slightest of doubt or even an atom's worth of doubt can be a major barrier in achieving your goals. Some people still achieve their goals despite doubt but they never get to experience their true potential, whereas some people with even the slightest of doubt will really struggle to achieve their goals.

I remember when I wrote my very first book, even though I believed in the techniques I was writing about because of the transformation it brought to my life, there was doubt on how the information was going to be received. Due to my doubt of how the information was going to be received, it took much longer to get the book written and published.

Although I was quite excited when the book was finally published, I had a lot of doubt that the book was going to be well received. The result was that the doubt caused me not to market the book properly and therefore there were hardly any sales of the book. At the time I did not realise how the doubt was affecting me, blaming it on other circumstances to the point where I even started doubting the techniques that once worked so well for me.

Once I was able to identify that it was my own doubt that was causing the failure in both the techniques that once worked and the sale of the book, I had to redefine the language going on in my head and start believing in my techniques again. Once I had achieved that, I had to once again redefine the language in my head about how the information will be perceived or accepted by others.

It was only after I had cleared my doubts did the book start selling and the feedback I received was generally positive. The reality is that not everyone is going to like what you have to say or offer, not everyone will relate to you or what you want to teach or sell them.

Once you can accept that you do not need the whole world or everyone around you to like you, that there will always be those who like you and those who are just not interested or don't like you, you can start to eliminate that self-doubt, it is not about what others think or say but about what you aim to achieve and how much you believe in yourself.

Self-doubt can really cause you to stop believing in yourself, your ideas and even believing that you really can achieve your dreams. It does not matter how big or small the doubt is, it will affect you on a subconscious level where you have very little or no control. It is that little self-doubt that will prevent you from seeing just how amazing or powerful you really are.

Have you ever had an amazing idea and when you shared that idea with a group of friends, almost everyone in that group were very quick to tell you why that idea will never work? In that moment you started doubting that idea eventually leading to you not pursuing that idea, it just ended up being brushed aside without you even taking a little action.

A few years later someone else has the same idea and it really worked for them leaving you kicking yourself for not acting upon your idea. Usually when you have a good idea and you share it with a group of friends or people around you, they will tell you it will not work based on their own fears and nothing else.

Those who tell you that something will not work without having even tried with their own ideas, are usually afraid to try something themselves and try and pass that fear on to you. The truth is they are telling you it does not work based only on their own fear and speculation without being able to present any facts or information proving that it will work or not. Your doubt creeps in based on the fears of others and not on fact, and it is this self-doubt that keeps you stuck where you are.

When it comes to acting upon a new idea or dream that you want to achieve, there are only two unknowns and nothing else. The first unknown is that you don't know if it will work. The second unknown is that you don't know if it will not work. Therefore the idea of something working or not is based on speculation and not proven fact. You cannot claim an idea does not work if you have not tried it; the reality is that it is only the self-talk that is either causing you to doubt or procrastinate on being in action with the new idea.

You got that idea for a reason and it is up to you and only you to decide whether you are going to act upon it or not. There are only two answers here; either yes or no, everything else is just an exaggerated story and due to this story, your answer may as well be "No I will not act on it"; "I will just stay where I am". When you listen to people talk about their ideas or someone suggests something that could transform their life, most people will say "Yes but" and all the justifications and excuses why it will not work comes up.

The moment you put a "but" in that sentence; you might as well say "I am not willing to do that". For example; when a person says "I want to be my own boss but I don't think it will work out for me" or "I don't know how to manage or run a business". In this case there was a positive idea, however the moment the "but" came into it the positive idea was cancelled out.

It is not about the how are you going to get there or how is it all going to happen? When you start to analyse the "How am I going to do it?" or "When will it all happen?" you will create doubt and fear causing you to give up on the idea claiming it does not work or blaming circumstances. Trying to figure out the "how" is the same as creating an exaggerated story that blocks you from moving forward. Generally most people get stuck in that exaggerated story going on in their heads. Breaking through that story takes courage and some work on your part as old habits, behaviours or past programmed attitudes will keep coming up automatically.

Getting what you want

The process is simple; first identify what you really want and this may take some thinking and contemplating for some people. Once you know what you really want, declare it in words, for example "I want to be my own boss". Keep the statement short, precise and to the point of what it is you really want. The next step is to be able to imagine the end result of your desire, goal and dream.

Try to get a sense of what it would look, feel and sound like when you have achieved that goal or dream. Once you have that end result clearly defined and your emotions around that feel good, state it in words in the positive and present tense as if you have already achieved it, remember to keep the sentences precise and to the point.

The next step is to ask yourself "What do I have right now to get started". Once you keep your focus on what you have right now to get started, you start creating the "how" without the exaggerated stories and doubts; you will be amazed at how many ideas you will come up with by just focusing on what you have right now to get started.

When you have all those ideas of what you can do to get started, write them down in order of priority or the ones you believe will get you started quicker. During this time try and be aware of the words you are using when writing down those goals of getting into action or started. The words you use must feel positive and powerful to you as the goal and dream is unique to you.

The one thing to remember is when you are writing down your goals, be aware of your emotions as they can create a disconnect or incongruence with what you want to achieve. When you write, no matter what you are writing about, you are writing from a subconscious level and it reflects what you are thinking or feeling in your handwriting.

You don't have to think how to write or formulate the letters; it all flows naturally when you write. Therefore you are writing from a subconscious level, even if you write down something that is positive but you are feeling negative or doubting the goal, the pessimism will reflect in your handwriting causing you to procrastinate when it comes to actually getting started.

When you are consciously writing down your thoughts and ideas, the style and formulation of letters in what you write is an ideomotor response from your subconscious mind on how you really feel about the goal or dream. You are not trained to analyse your own handwriting unless you are a graphologist, therefore it is important that when you are writing your goals and dreams that you create congruency by ensuring that you feel emotionally positive toward the goal, you have cleared all doubt of achieving that goal and that the sentences you write are simple, clear and to the point with regards to the goal.

Self-talk can really create a powerful barrier that will stop you from getting started with goals or things that need to be done in almost every area of your life, and most of the time the self-talk is based on past events and experiences. It is within this self-talk that perceptions and judgements are created, especially about others or how things are happening in the world.

Generally past experiences cause you to create habits and behaviours that do not work for you in the present time, therefore your present and future is determined or created by your past. This means that everything you do today, tomorrow or a few years from now going into the future will cause results that are similar or exactly like the results of the past. Each day will feel the same as yesterday and the cycle will just continue in the same way until you take action in reconstructing that language going on in your head.

The past is gone; you cannot physically walk into your past to change it, the only existence of this past is programmed into your subconscious and held there in memory. Memory is language and that language has programmed your habits and behaviours. You cannot delete memory but you can through your language modify your habits and behaviours that will stop you from doing things the same way over and over again. The definition of insanity is doing the same things over and over again while expecting different results.

Modifying Habits and Behaviours

When past events or experiences cause the habits or behaviours we have today, those habits and behaviours are programmed into our subconscious mind and it becomes an identity on the subconscious level. When you try to modify the habits or behaviours programmed into the subconscious mind, it is like trying to take away its identity and therefore it will resist.

The way to modify habits and behaviours is over a specific period of time and this will differ from person to person. The time frame generally is twenty one days to three months before the subconscious can fully accept the new behaviour or language. This is done for ninety consecutive days without missing a day in between. The moment you miss a day, it will be like starting from day one again. Remember that your habits and behaviours as well as your current language on your mind has been there for a fair amount of years, therefore this is not going to be easy, if it were easy, we would all be living the life we really wanted.

Fritz Pearls the founder of Gestalt Therapy states that the decisions we make in the present time is based on a cluster of memories from the past. Generally speaking this means that every time we start something new like a goal or personal development, our decisions on how we are going to perform or take action towards that goal is usually based on past experiences or memories. The old habits and behaviours will show up in our performance when attempting the new goal causing us to have some resistance towards achieving those goals and giving us similar results from our past.

The aim is to let go of emotional attachments to those past memories and create a new language that will help us to develop new attitudes and behaviours for achieving the new goal. Think about this for a moment; how many times have you wanted to start something new and when it came to asking someone for some assistance, you had the "what if's" going on in your head?

For example; "What if they say no?" or "What if they laugh at my idea?" and so on. Sometimes people, based on these past cluster of memories, will create stories deciding for the other person before they have even asked for assistance. When you create this perception and create the "what if's", it is like you have decided already that it will not work and chances are you will not get the assistance you need.

Think about it in another way. Have you ever had the experience where you have to attend a function and you know that there are specific people you don't like are going to be there? You create this whole scenario and story in your head of how bad the function is going to be for you, however when you get there, it is not half as bad as you thought it would be. If you did not have a nice time anyway it is probably due to the negative energy you created in that story in your head long before you got there. Next time you have to attend a function you think you might dread, try changing the language in your head of how you are going to enjoy the function and ignore all the negative conversations and see what happens.

Due to these clusters of past memories we create perceptions of situations or events that don't really represent the actual event or situation but based on how we think the situation is, which in reality it is an exaggerated story of the actual event. Richard Bandler a psychologist and John Grinder a professor of linguistics were the founders of Neuro Linguistic Programming (NLP). They state that the words we use reflect an inner, unconscious perception of our beliefs. If those words and perceptions are inaccurate, they will cause an underlying problem as long as we continue to use them.

These words and perceptions reflect our attitudes and in a sense, our attitudes are a self-fulfilling prophecy. Furthermore they state that all behaviour has a structure that can be modified, modelled, learned, taught and changed. Richard Bandler and John Grinder also describe perception as the internal representations that we make about an event are not necessarily the event itself; it is our perception of the event that we project outwardly.

This means that we run all those external events through our internal processing and then we make an internal representation of each event. This internal representation then combines with our physiology which creates the emotions we feel toward each event, such as happy feelings, sadness or motivated.

Our internal representations are all the pictures, sounds, dialog and feelings combined with our physiology or neurological systems. All external events that we experience come in through our five senses, sight, sound, smell, taste and touch, which are the channels through which we create the internal representations. The information coming into the conscious mind is filtered and then we process the information internally. As we process this information internally, we delete, distort and generalize all that information according to any number of elements.

We take in millions of pieces of information through our five senses throughout the day. The conscious mind cannot handle all these millions of pieces of information coming in and therefore it is held in the filter faculty of the conscious mind. When we process the information of the external event or experience, we first delete which means that we selectively pay attention to certain aspects of our experience and filter out the rest.

This leads to distortion where we create shifts in the sensory data of the experience causing a mis-representation of reality. We then generalize the event and then base this generalization on all events which is not reality or actual events. It is due to this deletion, distortion and generalization which are perception, that we make our decisions on all future prospects or events.

Really speaking this means that we base all our actions on a generalized and distorted view of what the reality is or could have been. We then create time, space or boundaries based on these perceptions which become our limitations in life. We can actually feel these limitations in our energy, if we see situations in less favourable or a negative light, our energy is generally low.

If we have a positive outlook toward something or life, our energy is usually high. Within this perception we also create unconscious values or beliefs especially related to things that matter to us. According to Richard Bandler beliefs are generalizations of how the world is. Beliefs are those things we cannot get around, beliefs are the on or off switch for our ability to do anything in the world.

In short your belief is what you perceive to be true is what you will project onto others or into the world. We also have values and attitudes which are created through perception or what is known as our value filters. This is how we decide whether our actions are good, bad, right or wrong, and they are also how we decide on how we feel about our actions. Attitudes are created from a combination of our memories and the decisions we make in life, created in how we think and feel about our beliefs and how we express these beliefs.

Richard Bandler states that values are those things that we don't have a tendency to live up to, values are typically what move people toward or away from stuck situations. Therefore it is plain to see that perception is what causes us to have that self-talk which does not benefit us in any way what so ever.

When we listen to others speak, we listen with these filters or internal representations, creating perceptions of what we think they are saying. When we listen with our perception or belief of our view of the world, we never really hear what the other person is saying and create a misrepresented view of what they are actually saying. We go into our internal dialog and create the decision of whether we agree with them or not. It is also our internal dialog that causes us to give the responses or advice that we give, which may not be what the other person really needs.

When you stop that internal dialog, hold back your perception of the other person and just listen to each word they say, repeating back to them exactly what they said, they will find their own solutions to what they need. Each one of us has the answers to our own problem, it is the internal dialog and perceptions we have in our heads that prevent us from seeing those answers. It is for this reason that most people have conflict with each other, they are constantly listening with their own perception and have to be right and project their belief onto the other person.

Sometimes if a person makes one mistake, that mistake is generalized and whenever there is something to be done or said, we listen to the other person based on that generalized view thinking they will always be that way in the way they do things. Ever had an experience where you have made a mistake and the other person then brings up every other mistake from the past even if those mistakes have got nothing to do with the current event? Have you ever been upset with someone and you bring up everything from the past because you believe that the current mistake has got everything to do with every other past event even if it is unrelated?

You do this because your perception has caused a single vision global view of the attitude of the other person. This all occurs in the language of your memory and self-talk, nothing else. Once you are able to change that perception through the words you use in your internal dialog, you will come to realise your power of choice, you can really choose how you want to feel and be in the world. You don't have to fix the other person, there is nothing to fix, all you have to do is change the language in your head and break through those emotional barriers and the world will change for you.

Each individual has the power to change their world by changing themselves.

The words you use, that internal dialog or language going on in your head from the time you were in your teenage years, has caused your life to be what it is today. It may not have occurred exactly like the way you speak it in your head but it is very close or similar to what is going on in that internal dialog, a form of self-fulling prophesies all created by you.

Everything that goes on in our life, the people we attract into our life, the circumstances we find ourselves in as we move into adulthood are all created in this internal language. The subconscious mind does not differentiate whether you have had a hard and difficult childhood or grew up in a very privileged home, we all create that internal dialog in the same way and we all have different outcomes.

No two people will ever have the same experience due to their perceptions. For example if two friends were to go on holiday to the same resort, spend every waking minute together and participate in the same events at the same time, when they come back from the holiday and write about the holiday, you will have two totally different stories even if the holiday at the resort was exactly the same.

In the same way if two people were to have the exact same goal, there would still be two different outcomes. The reason is that each person has taken action on those goals based on their own perception and belief of how they project themselves in the world. Some people go through a number of relationships, each one ending up being the same as the last one, even though the people and circumstances in each relationship was different.

They just keep attracting the same relationship over and over again no matter how much they dream of the perfect relationship. This is all caused by the internal dialog and emotional connection to the first relationship, unless they learn to completely let go of that first relationship and be willing to change their behaviour in how they view themselves in the relationship, they will continue attracting the same situations over and over again.

Life is really meant to be simple as the subconscious mind responds well to simple language; however our lives become complicated because we were brought up in the complicated language, beliefs and indoctrination of our elders, we then complicate it further with our own self-talk and continue the cycle with no end in sight.

We all go through challenging moments in our lives. Some people have extreme challenges, some even traumatic, while others have much less challenges, it is just how life is even if it seems very unfair, and really speaking there is little we can do about it right now. Whether we have had traumatic or extreme challenges, whether it was just difficult or somewhat light challenges, all these events are stored in memory on our subconscious mind.

Dealing with Fear

Every time we think of those past events an emotion is triggered and within this emotion lies fear. Sometimes we have moments where there are similar situations that resemble that past event causing our subconscious mind to trigger the fear of those past events. The fear we experience in the present time is not fear of what we are actually experiencing in that given moment but a triggered fear from the past memory.

Fear is False Expectation of Appeared Reality. This means when we are faced with a challenging situation or want to achieve something in the present time, we sometimes have fear towards that situation or achieving that goal based on a past experience. We create a false expectation of the outcome of the current situation or goal based on an appearance of what that reality could look like.

The appeared reality is usually an exaggerated story or vision in our mind and usually is not the outcome we were expecting. Fear is not something that can be easily overcome especially if it arose from a past experience that was traumatic or very difficult. Most people cannot get over fear on their own and require help from others such as psychologists or coaches. The truth is with the right help any fear can be overcome.

Some people are even afraid to ask for help, creating stories in their head of what people will think of them if they do. It is all stories and nothing else, you cannot read another person's mind or know what they are thinking. There will be those who are willing to help and there will be those who are not.

There is nothing wrong with asking for help and you will be surprised that there are more people than you can imagine that are willing to lend a helping hand. All you have to do is ask, even if one or two people cannot help you, keep asking as there is always help available. There are times when even people who are coaches or teachers require help dealing with certain aspects of their own lives.

It is impossible to know everything and even more difficult when we try and do everything ourselves. Releasing fear is not easy but can be done fairly quickly if you choose to face it and work on it. It mostly requires changing the language around the memory of past events and detaching yourself emotionally from the event itself.

Positive and negative emotions cannot be in the same place at the same time, the first step is to change your emotions toward the past event by telling yourself that the event is in the past and I cannot physically go there anymore. That past event only exists in my mind and is only affecting me right now because of triggered emotions and memories.

The next step is to identify whether it is a fear or a phobia. A phobia is something that triggers your fear but you have no idea or clue on how you got that fear, for example; you are scared of pigeons but have no idea where, when, how or any rational explanation on how that phobia started. Fear is when you know what actually caused it and when it started. For example; if you are scared of dogs and know that as a child you were bitten by a dog and since then every time you see a dog, you get scared, there is a where, when, how or rational explanation on how that fear started.

Although some fears are very difficult to deal with and require the help of professional coaches or psychologists, they can be overcome as they only exist in thought and memory. You can either choose to focus on those thoughts that keep triggering your fear or you can choose to focus on thoughts that empower you.

When you focus on thoughts that make you feel good and empowered, calling up all emotions related to those thoughts, you will start to feel positive and empowered. As the positive empowering emotions start to rise, you will notice that the fear starts to get less and less, you keep calling up those positive emotions until you cannot feel the fear anymore.

Fear and empowerment cannot be felt at the same time so you have the power to choose how you feel. It is really that simple but takes a lot of practice as it is easy to get triggered back into that old emotion again. The more you practice at calling up positive thoughts and emotions, the stronger and more powerful you will feel no matter what the current circumstances may be.

I encourage everyone to try and get some coaching in this area because trying to achieve everything on your own does not allow you to fully experience your true power and ability. Remember your disempowering self-talk has been going on in your head for a number of years, getting help allows us to identify the blind spots that keep us blocked because we are just not able to see them.

Fear can also be triggered by the thoughts of failure. The truth is that there are no such things as failure. Failure only exists in your life in two ways, in your head through the conversations you are having about failure or your unwillingness or failure to take action. When you try something it is either going to work or not. If it does not work, that does not mean you have failed, what it really means is that you tried something and it did not work and there could have been a number of factors that could have caused it not to work.

The fact that you tried something is power in itself, this means you have gained experience and not failed even if it does not work out for you. Sometimes we will all make silly or stupid decisions in our lifetime, there will be times where we make the wrong decision or choices, it really happens to everyone and we are not alone in making those choices or decisions.

There may be consequences to those decisions but it does not mean we have failed, we have two choices, and that is we can either learn from it or allow it to beat us down for the rest of our lives. When we choose to learn from it and not verbally beat ourselves up about those decisions, we create a new language that will help us get up again and work towards trying something new that can transform our lives.

Dealing with Procrastination

Procrastination is failure to take action and is based in language as well. When you procrastinate; you are really creating excuses and justifications on why you cannot start or take action, it is the voice chatting in your head that you are constantly listening to that makes you distract yourself from being in action toward transforming your life. The trick is to decide what you want and what you have right now to get started. When you have identified what you have to get started, stop thinking and choose to take action immediately, the moment you let the thoughts run, you will go into procrastination mode. Switch off that negative language in your head and use your power of choice to start being in action immediately.

At first this will be hard to do, however with everything in life; it takes some practice to get right. The aim is to train your mind to believe that you can do it, that it is really possible for you to achieve what you want and that you deserve it. If you have had experiences in the past where things have not worked for you, you can stop that fear by allowing yourself to look back at those situations and see what positive things you can learn from those situations.

Change the language about yourself, stop the self-beating talk and really honour yourself with kind words. Start with positive affirmations that resonate with you, for example "I am powerful and strong".

There are many such affirmations to choose from, the best affirmation is the one you create for yourself that truly resonates with you.

Keep that affirmation short and simple so you don't always have to think hard of what it is all the time. Be kind to yourself in the words you use on yourself and look back at the past as something to learn from and be able and willing to let go and leave it where it belongs; in the past.

Another aspect that creates the conversations of failure is comparing you to others. When you start looking at others and how well they are doing, sometimes causing a bit of jealousy, you creating a language that says "I am not good enough". There will be times when you and someone you know may have the same goal but they succeed at it and you don't.

That does not mean you have failed, it could have been that it was not really your goal but chose to achieve it because you had no other ideas of what to do at the time. There was a lack of passion in achieving that goal; chances are that you chose that goal because it sounded good being someone else's idea. All that means is that you doubt your own ideas and it is that self-doubt that will cause things to not work out the way you want them to.

Sometimes you may want to aspire to be like someone whom you see as your hero, trying to emulate them in every way possible and it does not work out. The truth is you cannot be anyone other than yourself. The most powerful person you can be is none other than yourself. It does not matter how big or small your goals are, you don't have to base your success on what others are doing, think or say. You define what success means to you based on what you are passionate about.

The truth is that it does not matter how many accolades, awards, recognition or money other people have, you cannot be them, what matters most is what you are passionate about and how you define that in your language. You become really successful at what you do when you first define it in language and are able to feel and act as if you are already there, without worrying about what others are going to say or think or whether you make more money or have more fame.

You will find real fulfilment in what you do when you choose to define who you really are and base your success on your ideas and passion, believing in yourself without doubt. When you can create the language of "I know I can achieve whatever I want to achieve", you can create a language on your subconscious that will help you believe that anything is possible and that you know you can achieve the things that you are passionate about, you are really that powerful.

Changing self-talk is not going to be easy, it really is hard work and most people will run away from hard work especially if it concerns dealing with themselves in ways they have never done before. It is so much easier to allow the negative talk to take over, cast blame on others and circumstances rather than to take responsibility.

Most people are afraid of that responsibility because it means being responsible for everything that has happened in their life whether they were at fault or not, whether they were right or wrong. It does not matter what your life has been like until now, what matters is the choice you have in front of you.

You can choose to continue living in that world which is based on past programmed habits and behaviours that are not serving you in the present time, you can choose to continue blaming the world for what is wrong in it or in your life or you can take back your power and choose to be responsible for everything in your life, all the positive and negative parts of your life without judgement.

Only you can choose what you really want if it is going to work for you. Once you choose to be responsible and be in action with transforming your life you can start with little bits at a time by changing your language about yourself. It is like looking in the mirror and telling the person in the mirror that he or she does matter and has a positive role to play in this world. You can start by creating kind and loving words about yourself no matter what your current circumstances are.

You will find that in the beginning you will resist this and automatically go into that negative conversation in your head, it is up to you to become aware of that and immediately change the language to kind and loving words about yourself. Therefore in short; the best way to transform the self-talk and let go of all those past negative language, habits, behaviours and attitudes is to create kind and loving words about yourself that makes you feel good and fully accepting of who you are in the current moment.

Once you have that full acceptance of self with no attachments to the past and anything else, your new language that you create will be your pathway to transforming yourself into a powerful human being where anything can be possible to achieve. When you transform yourself, the world will transform to accommodate you.

Self-talk has another aspect that almost everyone is so unaware of. When you receive a compliment or acknowledgement, how do you feel? Do you get awkward? Do you blush? Do you try and brush it off and quickly change the topic? Whatever the reaction to receiving a compliment may be, almost everyone has those similar experiences unless the individual is self-absorbed and egotistic.

Do you respond to compliments in the way you do because you don't want to come across as being egotistic? Or afraid the other person will see you as having a swollen head? Do you genuinely feel those awkward moments? The reason for this is also based in an unconscious language. Something from your past causes you to feel "I am not good enough". It could have been in your childhood when you thought you had done something wonderful and were expecting to receive a compliment for it; instead you got criticized or shouted at because it was seen as wrong by the adults around you.

This "I am not good enough" becomes a stored negative emotion. When someone compliments you, there is an ideomotor response from the subconscious mind of those past events of not being good enough. This then causes you to have difficulty to receive those compliments. It is difficult to see yourself in that light.

The truth is that someone compliments you because they genuinely see something special there. To break those negative emotions of "I am not good enough" and "I don't deserve", you have to train yourself to receive those compliments. It is not going to be easy but it can be done quickly with practice by changing the language going on in your head in that moment.

The first step you have to remember is to first smile and thank the person for the compliment and then in your mind, say "I acknowledge you (say your name) for this". Practice acknowledging yourself in this manner. Train yourself to believe that you do deserve this recognition. By thanking the person and then quietly acknowledging yourself in your mind, you are not feeding your ego.

If it does feel as if you are feeding your ego, tell yourself "thank you for what you did, it has made a difference in someone's life". Acknowledging yourself while stating the difference it makes for someone else will bring more fulfilment and allow you to break through those barriers of "I am not good enough" or "I don't deserve. This is something you will have to practice and give it time; you will notice a huge difference in your life when you are able to receive those compliments without the body sensations and without feeding the ego.

When you want to work on self-development or have a goal that you want to achieve, have you ever told yourself that you are not ready? If you have said "I am not ready to do that right now", you then put it off for as long as you can. The reality is that nobody is ever ready.

Think about this for a moment. When someone dies and you have to attend their funeral especially if it is in another city, do you call them up and tell them to wake up and die another day? You are not ready to travel and be at their funeral? When there is a car accident, do you tell the other driver to rewind and cause the accident on another day because you were not ready for this accident?

If there is an armed robbery, do you tell the armed robbers to come back another day because you were not ready? If someone in your family suddenly gets sick and you have to rush them to hospital, do you tell them to get sick another day because you are not ready to take them to the hospital now?

These are all traumatic events that happen in people's lives every day. Nobody is ready for any of that.

However once it happens you are then forced to take certain actions immediately to deal with the situations. You don't sit and think what to do but just get into action, for example rushing the family member to hospital. In the same way for less traumatic events, in this case learning and practicing a new self-development technique or language to transform your life.

Ask yourself why don't you ever get started immediately? If you tell yourself you are not ready, you will never be ready. Unfortunately life just works that way. We have to be forced into situations before we start taking action. It is like you know that the roof on the house must be fixed before the rain comes, you tell yourself you will get to it soon but when the rain comes, you suddenly find yourself in action fixing the roof.

Human beings constantly wait for a situation to arise before they take real action. For this reason it is important that you make the choice now, do you practice what you learn here now or do you continue in that same old way for the rest of your life going nowhere?

The best way to transform yourself is to stop listening to that self-talk of I am not ready and force yourself to start taking action in your transformation. It can only come from you and no one else. Your transformation lies in your hands and there are no circumstances or people other than yourself to blame, the responsibility lies with you. Therefore the only way to move forward is to make the choice now of what you want. Do you want transformation? Do you want to stay stuck where you are right now?

Chapter 5
The Power of Your Words

Creating your power words will seem quite difficult at first for one simple reason; you have been programmed to be the way you are currently for a number of years. Your subconscious mind will need some time to process and accept the new words or language for transformation. The words that you speak whether aloud or in your mind carry a lot of power and can influence how your subconscious mind will respond to different situations.

Creating your new language is a conscious choice and will require some effort on your part especially in the beginning because it is very easy to fall back into that automatic mode of the old habits and behaviours. There will be a lot of resistance during this time and those voices in your head will try and convince you to quit.

You have the power of choice to either give in to those old programs or to really be willing to take on the task of self-transformation from a deeper level. As you have already learnt from chapter four; the first step is to use kind and loving words on yourself no matter what the current circumstances are.

There has to be a willingness on your part to really honour yourself so that you can start to trust and believe in yourself. It is only from this place of honouring yourself will you truly learn how powerful you really are. The aim is to start slowly and not be in a rush so that you can get the full benefit of the new language both from a conscious and unconscious level. The reality today is that society has been programmed to expect instant gratification and it is so easy to discard something within a few days if there are no signs of immediate results.

Unfortunately your subconscious mind does not work that way and requires a lot of patience on your part. Once you are able to get to that place where you truly honour yourself, believe and trust in yourself that you do have the power to create the life you want starting with your internal language, the results of achieving goals will get faster as you move forward and progress in the practice of creating powerful words or language that help you create attitudes and behaviours that get you into action.

The technique of creating a new language is very simple. Choosing how you want to feel and bringing up your energy is just as simple, it is letting go of the old habits and emotions that is difficult. Being constantly aware of your words is not going to be easy as you will fall back into that old language very quickly due to the unconscious resistance.

You will have to really train yourself to be constantly aware of those words going on in your head. It will take some courage to really challenging yourself to break through those emotional barriers, get into working on yourself, creating and sustaining the new language. The challenge will be worth it because as you develop that new language of transformation, you will learn just how powerful you can really be and that anything you put your mind to is possible to achieve.

What the mind conceives it will achieve. The important thing to remember is that by just changing your language is not going to just make things happen magically, you still have to set your goals and take action toward achieving them. The new language will help to break through those barriers of self-doubt and procrastination. Everything in life starts in language therefore even being negative or procrastination only exists in that self-talk going on in your head.

The trick is to define what you want and not to think about how you are going to achieve it but what you are able to do to get started and just be willing to take action. When you get into that thinking and analysing mode, the voices in your head start popping up sending you into that self-talk that stops you from being in action. When you have clearly defined what you want, create an image of the end result, what will it look like when you have achieved that goal.

To create a further enhancement of achieving that goal, you will need to create what is known as sensory acuity towards achieving that goal. This is done by being able to see and act as if you have already achieved that goal no matter what the current circumstances may be. You have to really feel and identify with that success before it has even happened to reduce the unconscious resistance that blocks you from achieving what you really want, the aim is to stop chasing the goal but creating it in language which is both verbal and non-verbal.

It is for this reason why many coaches will tell you that you have first got to learn to be happy now no matter what your circumstances. It is not the other person or money that is going to make you happy, the way you feel is a choice and you have the power to choose how you want to feel at any time you want.

Although transformation begins with using words of kindness and honouring yourself, the truth about self-development is that it is not something that you can fully achieve on your own. You have probably heard the saying thousands of times that no human being is an island. There is so much truth in that statement especially when it comes to self-development and transformation.

There are people in this world who have achieved success on their own; however it is usually only success in one or two areas of their life. People who have achieved tremendous success in their careers have usually neglected areas of their life such as relationships and health.

Self-development and Transformation

It does not matter how many books you have read on self-development or how many courses or workshops you have done, the hard truth is that you will not get the full benefit of self-development and transformation by yourself. The reason for this is that it is so easy to give into the resistance or the voice going on in your head because there is nobody available to hold you accountable to your intentions and actions.

I am not just talking about working with a coach. To get the full benefit of self-development and transformation requires forming a group of five or six people, a maximum of ten, who are also working on self-development for themselves. The purpose of being part of a group is so that you can create a support structure that will help each other achieve the maximum benefit of transformation in the areas of your lives that all of you are working on.

This may not be easy for some, especially for those who have been doing things alone for a long time. When you have a group that you can work and communicate with, not only are you creating a support structure but you have the advantage of having people who can point out areas that you could be missing or not recognising in your transformation, sort of the blind spots or areas you are unable to see yourself.

Self-development and transformation is about being honest and authentic with yourself and in the same way you have to bring that honesty and authenticity to the group. Most people will struggle with this idea because most people shy away from the truth for the fear of looking bad and what others may think.

Transformation is not about how good or bad you look but about how honest you can be with yourself and others in every aspect of your life, the good and the not so good parts of you. Working with a group will help you bring integrity and honesty to yourself and will train you to keep your promises or word, not only to yourself but to others as well.

If there is no integrity in what you do, you are just fooling yourself when it comes to your own transformation. If you truly want to be helpful to others, you first have to learn to help yourself in every area of your life and the only way to get the full benefit of that is to work with likeminded people in small groups.

If this is not resonating with you right now for whatever reason, that is okay. You have that power of choice. It will take some time for you to fully accept the idea of working with others especially when it comes to dealing with your life. Once you can break through those barriers that hold you back from sharing and being with others in self-development, you will start to see the greater power of the whole process.

There will be times when you will have some strong body sensations and emotions when working on transforming yourself. Although I mentioned that it all begins with you stating kind words and honouring yourself, there will be times when you will have to stand in front of the mirror and really be stern with yourself. Some people will have to really shout at themselves to pull themselves together.

Those emotions and body sensations are high unconscious resistance which is like stepping out from the known into the unknown, like taking an identity away from the subconscious. In these instances it will require a lot of courage and strength on your part to really be strong and stern with yourself if you really want that transformation.

Remember you have the power of choice. You can either give in to those old habits and behaviours or you can choose to cause your transformation. The good news is that when you have a negative emotion going on, you can change it quite quickly by choosing power words and really allow yourself to feel the emotions of those power words.

Negative and Positive Emotions cannot Exist in the Same Place

Negative and positive emotions cannot exist in the same place at the same time. For example if you are feeling frustrated because things are not working the way you want them to, first accept that emotion, give it a number from one to ten, with ten being the worst and zero being no feeling at all. Do not think of a number toward the frustrated feeling, just trust your subconscious mind and accept the first number that comes into your head.

Once you have a number, for example seven, start stating powerful words like "I feel empowered", "I am powerful", or "I can achieve anything I set my mind to" and so on while really getting yourself to feel those words. You keep stating and feeling those power statements until it feels as if those negative feelings have completely gone. When your emotions are in the positive state and quite high, you will be amazed at how many solutions you will come up with to overcome that frustration of things not going the way you want them to.

Creating your Power Words

When it comes to creating your power words or affirmations, the best ones are the ones that you create. The reason for this is that when you create your own power words or affirmations, you can create them from a deep subconscious level, bypassing your filter faculty which allows your subconscious to accept the new words and positive language much quicker than having to learn and memorise those created by others.

I can give you thousands of words and affirmations; unfortunately the reality is, I have never met you, I don't know you therefore I cannot evaluate your current programming and the language that you currently use on yourself. The truth is that every human being has access to all the answers of their life within them. It is the blind spots or the way our current habits and behaviours are programmed that does not allow us to see those answers.

Every human being has a high level of creativity within them; all you need is to be guided in the direction that will help you discover this power within. Creating your own power words and affirmations are not as difficult as you may think. A good time to create your power words or affirmations is when you are alone sitting quietly and in a deep relaxed state. Otherwise the best time is fifteen minutes before you go to sleep, that time when you feel like you can doze off at any moment.

During this time of drowsiness your filter faculty has shut down and your conscious mind is not processing or reasoning at that moment, this means you have direct access to your subconscious mind. The other time is in the morning when you have just woken up, your filter faculty and conscious mind takes some time to wake up so you have direct access to your subconscious mind. During this time, you can create suggestions for your subconscious mind to overcome procrastination and help you be in action with what you need to do.

Meditation Technique

Meditation is another good technique to use to create your power words and affirmations because when you are in the meditative state, your body is completely relaxed and your conscious mind and filter faculty are shut off. I am not speaking of meditation for spirituality or yoga; I am talking about light and simple forms of meditation where you get to a relaxed state with the mind clear. These forms of meditation can be done sitting on a chair or lying down, whatever is most comfortable for you.

You can get yourself relaxed by just sitting in a comfortable position and breathing deeply in and out through your nose. You can then further enhance the relaxation by choosing words that you relate to in-order to help you further relax. You will need to repeat this exercise daily to help you create that state of relaxation and be associated with it on a subconscious level. The following words are just a few words that you can choose from to help you get relaxed. You only need to choose one word that you can relate to.

Relax	Peace
Relaxation	Calmness
Lightness	Joy
Floating	Happiness
Loose	Contentment
Tingling	Harmony

You can choose one of the words in the list, however if you have other words that you can strongly relate to, then it is best to choose those words as they are closely associated to you on a subconscious level. When you have the word that you can relate to, try and repeat that word as many times as possible when relaxing.

Once your subconscious mind becomes associated with the word and you relaxing, eventually you will only need to say that word and your body will automatically go to that relaxed state, you still breathe deeply in and out of your nose to create the alpha state to help you get directly to the subconscious level. The association with the word and your body getting relaxed usually takes around twenty one to Thirty days; this is after practicing for thirty consecutive days without missing a day in-between.

Like the above exercise, where you chose one word to be associated with you relaxing or getting into a relaxed state, you can choose one word that will help you feel powerful, energetic or create the feeling of being in action. However before choosing this power word, it would be a good idea to identify how you perceive information. Are you a visual person and usually associate images with conversations? Notice if you relate to the following words to help you create your power words.

See	I see what you are saying	I see it is
View	In view of	Bird's eye view
Appears	It appears to be	An appearance of
Look	Looks like	Looks good to me
Imagine	I imagine it to be	I can imagine it will
Sight	You are a sight for sore eyes	I have it in my sight
Clear	It is clear to me now	I see it clearly
Envision	I envision it to be	I have a vision of

If you relate to the above set of words and short statements, you are most likely a visual type of person and therefore should choose words that make you look empowered, energised and confident. You are usually able to see the big picture and therefore words like powerful, strong, whole, perfect and happy will relate to you and you will be able to imagine yourself as that.

When starting with your power words you start by saying "I see myself as powerful" while imagining and visualising what being empowered looks and feels like. The next step is to bring it down to the single word like "empowered" and be able to visualize what it would look and feel like to be empowered, this is done every day for ninety days until your subconscious creates an association with being empowered every time you say the word empowered or powerful.

Do not worry about trying to get it right, there is no right or wrong way to do this, all that is required is for you to create an association with words that make you feel positive and empowered every time you say that specific word that you relate to. The unique word must come from you as you are a unique individual and therefore would be able to create that power word from a deeper level of your subconscious mind. This makes it easier to create that association that will help you be more positive about yourself.

If you are the type of person who cannot visualize easily or get the big picture, you need to know the details on how things are done or if you are easily distracted by noise, notice if you can relate to the following words and short statements.

Hear	I hear what you are saying	I heard voices
Listen	It is clearly expressed	Loud and clear
Resonate	Clear as a bell	I hear you
Sound	That sounds good to me	Sounds like a good idea
Tune	I'm tuned into that	I tuned out during the conversation
Tell	I am all ears	To tell the truth
Speak	In a manner of speaking	You speak my language
Clear	It is clear to me	I need more clarification

If you relate to the above words or short statements, it indicates that you are more of an auditory person. You would start creating your power words by stating "I want to be powerful". While stating that statement, try and create an emotion of feeling powerful until you start to actually feel powerful when stating the word powerful. You can change powerful to energetic, happy, strong or whole and perfect. The important thing is to choose words that sound good and positive to you.

If you are the type of person who feels deep emotion, needs to do things to understand how it works or likes to touch and get a feeling of things, notice how the following words and short statements relate to you.

Feel	I feel your presence	Your words feel good to me
Grasp	I have a grasp of it	I can't grasp that info right now
Catch	I got a catch on it	I caught on to the last bit
Touch	Your words touch me	I will touch base with you later
Handle	I got a handle on it	I cannot get a handle on this new info
Tap	I can tap into the conversation	I could not tap into what you said
Concrete	That feels solid to me	There is no concrete evidence
Solid	You have a solid plan	It does not feel like a solid idea to me

If you relate to the above words or short statements, this indicates that you are a Kinaesthetic type of person. This means you would start by stating "I feel powerful". The advantage you have is that you get to really tune into that emotion of being powerful.

You can really get a feel of words like energetic, perfect, strong, loving, harmonious and happy. You would choose words that really feel good to you. Once you have a feel of the word that resonates with you, for example "empowered", you repeat that word while feeling the emotion of being empowered until you actually feel empowered every time you just say the word empowered.

The exercise above is merely for indicative purposes only and may not be accurate. If you would like more information or a detailed explanation on how to identify whether you are a visual, auditory, kinaesthetic or auditory digital type or how you perceive information, you can do that by reading up on NLP by Richard Bandler and John Grinder.

The purpose of the information here is to help you get a better understanding of how the words or language that you use can affect the way you achieve your goals or be the cause of your circumstances. The idea is to help you understand that in order to overcome obstacles or stuck situations, you first have to identify the words and context sentences that you are currently using, and then change it to help you transform yourself or the way you do things.

This is not a new technique but an enhancement of what you already know, it is about going back to the beginning of the whole process of the self-help technique you are already using and changing the language to overcome the obstacles as everything in life is created in language.

If you are struggling to find your power words right now, don't beat yourself about it, some people do take a while before they get to that word that makes them feel empowered or energised. For now you can choose one of the words below until you find your own power word, however if you find that you can resonate with one of the power words below, you can continue to use that word.

When using your power words in a context sentence, use the prefix "I am" or "I live in", to enhance it on the subconscious level that will define you as being that powerful person. With some people the subconscious mind will process the words "power, powerful and empowered" in different contexts, therefore treat them as different words even though they have same or similar meanings. The same would apply for "energy, energetic or energized". It is not important to get caught up in the context of it, choose the one that pops in your head first or creates the most positive emotion.

Abundant	I am abundance	I live in abundance
Affluent	I am affluent	I live in affluence
Attract	I am power of attraction	I attract abundance of
Cause	I am the cause of my life	I live in causing my destiny
Create	I am the creator of...	I create my outcome
Deserve	I am deserving of...	I deserve the best
Destiny	I am my power of destiny	My destiny lies in my hands
Empowered	I am empowered	I live an empowered...
Energy	I am energised	I live in positive energy

Essence	I am the essence of...	I live in the essence of unlimited...
Great	I am greatness	I excel in the greatness of...
Happy	I am happy	I live in happiness
Harmony	I am harmony	I live a harmonious life
Intelligence	I am intelligence	I live in the power of intelligence
Intuition	I am intuitive	I have the power of intuition
Knowledge	I am all knowing	I know I can...
Light	I am the Light	I live in the light of abundance
Love	I am love	I radiate abundance of love
Manifest	I am manifestation of...	I manifest all that which I choose
Master	I am the master of my...	I master the ability to...
Power	I am powerful	I live in the power of...

Strong	I am strength	I live in the strength of...
Unity	I am united with my...	I live in the unity of creation
Unlimited	I am unlimited	I have unlimited...
Wealth	I am wealthy	I have a wealth of...

The above are some power words you can choose from with some possible context sentences you can create to start your positive language about yourself. The words "I am" really creates a powerful association with you becoming what you choose to create or be in the world or achieving your goals.

It helps create an identity with your subconscious mind to reduce resistance and help you achieve and manifest your dreams at a faster rate, however this will differ from person to person therefore it is important to have patients and not question when it will happen.

Chances are if things are not happening for you there is something missing in your language or you are still struggling to be in action. The important thing to remember is not to beat yourself up about things not working for you. The aim is to first create a positive language about yourself before you can create positive emotions that will help you achieve your goals and dreams.

If you really want things to manifest in your life, you first have to learn to love and respect yourself; create a powerful feeling within yourself no matter what your current circumstances may be. It is easy to get caught up in what is going on around us than it is to focus on what it is we really want. This is an exercise we really have to work on with a lot of courage; that is to stay focused on what we really want despite the obstacles and circumstances in our lives.

Everybody has a high degree of creativity. All it takes is to allow yourself to have at least thirty minutes a day of "me time" to get into a relaxed state so that you can open yourself up to that creativity, when you allow yourself to do that, you will be able to create an amazing powerful language that will move you forward in achieving what you want. You have to believe that you have the power to create and deserve, and believe that you can achieve whatever it is that you want.

Your context sentences should be precise and short as your subconscious mind responds better to direct suggestions. When you create statements that are too long, chances are you won't remember it or will struggle to create an association with it on the subconscious level, causing you to have conflict with what it is you are trying to achieve.

The statement must be stated in the positive as if you have achieved it already, for example "I am a powerful coach in communication", this statement states what you are and in the area you work in. It is short and precise and describes what you are while creating an identity on your subconscious level of who you choose to be.

The secret is that you have to be the successful person you want to be on a mental and emotional level long before you have achieved it. You have to be able to see yourself as that person and act as if it is already happening no matter what your current job may be. It does not matter what your financial circumstances may be, also what you are currently experiencing in your life, until you can create a mental image or act as if you are the successful person you choose to be, it will be very difficult to overcome the obstacles that hold you back.

To create success you have to change your thoughts and way of thinking to that of abundance, you have to be able to see the possibility of having what you want long before you have it. When your thoughts and conversations are based on lack, your life experience will be that of being in a place of lack. Your thoughts and emotions play a vital role in what or who you become, it is for this reason it is so important to disconnect from emotions and thoughts of the past if you want to succeed in the future.

If your thoughts are based on fears of past experiences, chances are they will reappear in your future as we live into our future based on the thoughts and language we have today. In short; if we keep thinking and speaking about the past, we live into that past as we go into the future.

There are some words that you want to avoid when creating your new language, context statements or affirmations. The subconscious mind does not recognize the word "don't" and therefore will omit it from the sentence, for example for the words "I don't want to struggle", the subconscious mind reads it as "I want to struggle", and creating those obstacles that will keep you struggling through life.

Most people are very good at knowing what they don't want. When you ask them what they really want in their life, usually most people will respond with "Well I don't want to struggle" or "I don't want to work in this dead end job". What their subconscious mind is reading is that they want to be where they are and creates more of what they don't want. Therefore it is important that you state exactly what you want in a short precise sentence that is stated in the positive and present tense, for example "I am financially free", or "I am loving the work I do".

The same would apply to the words "not" and "never", "I will not be negative" or "I will never do something like that". The subconscious will read it as "I will be negative" or "I will do something like that". You change those statements from "I will not be negative" to "I am a positive and powerful person". "I will never do something like that" to stating "I will live my life with integrity and honesty".

Sometimes when you see or observe something that is negative to you, the best thing is to ignore it if you cannot do anything about it unless it is something that is happening in your life in that moment. Choosing the right words may not come easy to some at first. The trick is to play around with words while creating positive statements that actually feel powerful and good to you. As explained before, the best words and statements are the ones you create as they resonate with your subconscious mind much more easily.

Unfortunately for some strange reason, and to our greater disadvantage, the subconscious mind will recognize the words "not", "don't" and "never" when we say things about ourselves personally. When you use words that put you down like "I don't deserve" or "I am not good enough", the subconscious accepts that literally and causes emotions that make you feel undeserving and not good enough.

This in turn stops you from choosing to be who you really are and that is a powerful human being that can achieve much more than you choose to recognize and see about yourself. Words like "I will never achieve anything in life" will occur exactly like that, you will never achieve. So whether we believe we are using the words "not", "don't" and "never" in a positive way it actually turns out negative and the opposite is true, those words will cause negativity to increase when using it to describe ourselves.

Another word that does not serve you is the word "need" even if you think you are using it in a positive way. The word "need" relates on the subconscious mind as always being in need of something. When you say "I need to get started on my project", chances are you will procrastinate for as long as you can before actually getting started. When you say "I need new clients", you will struggle to find clients as you tend to stay in that state of need. When you state "I need more money", chances are you will constantly be in that state of needing more money.

The word "need" must be replaced with the word "want" if you want your intentions to work for you, for example "I want to get started on my project", "I want new clients" and "I want more money". When you change the word to "want", you are creating a positive intention. However you cannot just leave it there and expect miracles to happen, once you have created the intention, "I want to get started on my project", you have to follow that up by taking action immediately or setting a date and time when you will start with that project.

You have to train yourself to keep to your promise of getting started with the project by sticking to the date and time you said you will start otherwise your subconscious will learn that keeping your promises is not necessary and will reflect that in most areas of your life. If you have become an unreliable person, it is because you cannot honour yourself by keeping your intentions and promises causing you to go through life without ever achieving something big. Every human being has the power to achieve something big if they are willing to be their word and take action on their intentions.

Everything you speak or say about yourself will be reflected onto your subconscious mind in some way at some point in time where it will show up in your life in some way. When you suddenly feel sick and you actually say "I feel sick" notice how you start to feel worse after you have said it. Instead it is better to start using words like "I know that I will heal from this quickly", "I am feeling better and better", "I heal at a rapid rate" and so on.

Keep using positive words on yourself no matter how sick you feel. It is not going to be easy; however the more you practice saying positive words to yourself the more you will start to feel healthy and strong. Negative things happen to all of us during our lifetime, if you want to transform that, the best way to do it is to accept that it has happened and it cannot be un-happened no matter what you say or do.

Avoid getting into those statements of "Why is this happening to me?" "If only I had done something else." "What if I had been somewhere else?" When you get caught up in those statements you create mental images of the events that get you emotionally attached to the event. This is when you create the exaggerated story of the event and then get stuck and cannot move forward.

If you can train yourself, which is probably going to be difficult to do at first, begin to look at the negative event and acknowledge it for what it is and not put right or wrong to it, not add a story to it or ponder on how you could have done things differently. Instead try to look at the event for what it is exactly and ask yourself what are the positives that I can learn from this event.

When you try and identify any positive learning from the negative event, you start training your mind to attract more positive things to you. It really is that simple but it is the emotional attachments and the not letting go that will hold you back and stuck in that past.

The next step is to forgive yourself for the negatives that have happened in your life, forgive yourself for holding on to that past event and saying all those negative things about yourself and allow yourself to let it go. This will be very hard to do in the beginning as you have trained yourself for so long to hold on to those past events, once you let go, you start emptying that space to create the life you really want.

Creating intentions or letting go of the past will be more powerful if you put it into a short precise statement and say it out loud to declare it. Sometimes it is good to state this declaration in front of one or more people to create more awareness and authenticity of what you are letting go of and what your new intention for your life is.

There will be times when you will have to make the statements stern as if you are commanding the new intention or commanding the past event to be gone. If you are letting go of a past event state it as clearly as possible, for example "I completely let go of that negative event in my life".

In your case you will need to state exactly what the negative event was, do not get caught up in the details of the event, just state what it was and leave it at that. Depending on how much the past negative event has affected you or how long you have been holding on to it, you may find that it still pops up into your mind. Do not let this bother you, just declare again that you completely let go of that event as many times as possible until you cannot feel any emotions toward that event.

Create a new intention you would like to focus on and declare it out loud. When creating your new intention you can start with "I intend to" for example "I attend to start my own consultant business". Once you have declared the intention, state it in the positive as if you are that consultant, for example "I am a digital marketing consultant". Then set the goal of being that consultant by writing it down.

The important thing to remember is that when you declare something, it is like making a promise to yourself that you want to achieve something. Just declaring it is not going to be enough. You will have to start taking action on it immediately otherwise you will be training yourself to keep breaking promises. The more you practice taking action on your declarations, you will start to create a powerful shift on moving away from procrastination and you will find that your procrastination will get less and less over time.

To sum it all up; every human being has the right answers within themselves, every human being has the power to achieve what they want to achieve. It is the mental blocks in our up-bringing or past events that block us from seeing these answers or recognizing that power.

Every human being is born intelligent, it is the social environment, parents, guardians, peers, culture and religious beliefs that we grow up in that program us to be what we are, blocking us from accessing that intelligence. It does not matter where or how we grow up, we can open that intelligence and find those answers with the right guidance. All it takes is to change the language about ourselves and the way we think and perceive ourselves to be.

You can start doing this by standing in front of the mirror and say three positive things about you every day. Accept your body for what it is even if right now you do not like it for whatever reason, then state three positive things about it each day. Over time you will start feeling good and positive about yourself and will start to feel powerful towards achieving your goals and dreams.

Really speaking you don't need another person to teach you about creating your new positive language, all you have to do is find one word that helps you relax or become calm and practice that word until you actually feel calm. The next step is to find one positive word that makes you feel good and use it in a sentence about yourself.

As you start saying positive things and statements about yourself, you will start creating a positive language in all areas of your life. There will be times when the negativity will overwhelm you and draw you back down, all you have to do is state something positive and you will start uplifting yourself.

There will be times when you will have to be stern with yourself and really push yourself forward, remember not to beat yourself up about it but change the language about yourself that will help you move forward. As you start with one positive statement; it will start to spiral from there and you will be surprised and amazed at just how you have the ability to create positive statements about yourself.

The best positive and powerful words and statements in your language about yourself are the ones that you create because there will be a close association with your subconscious mind that will allow those positive things to manifest in your life in a much powerful way. It is for this reason why everyone claims that you are the master of your own destiny. Nobody can create your destiny better than you can.

If you are feeling overwhelmed about how you are going to create your new language, stop worrying. All you have to do is start with one simple positive statement and build it up from there. When you declare what you want to achieve, keep imagining as if you have achieved it already, try and speak as if you are that successful person long before it has happened to create the sensory acuity you need to make it real and happen.

It is all about keeping it simple and short. It is the exaggerated language that makes things difficult. It is all about taking action without thinking what others are going to think or say, it is all about what you want. If the goal is based on someone else's goal, you may achieve it but you will never know how powerful and creative you can be.

When setting your goals ask yourself if it is for you and what you will achieve from the end result of the goal. You don't need to know how you are going to get there or the details on how it is going to be achieved, all you have to do is identify what you have now to get started and take action immediately, the "how" will take care of itself as you take the necessary actions.

Be kind to yourself with the words you use and accept there will be mistakes along the way, accept and acknowledge them, identify what you can learn from them and then move forward without delving on them. You do have the ability to choose how you want to feel, you can either choose to stay in that negative feelings or create statements that make you feel happy and positive, and it is that simple, you have the power to choose how you feel.

Everything can be a choice if you just choose it for what it is without reason or justification of it all. You are truly a powerful human being and all it takes for you to recognise that is to create positive statements about yourself and stay focused on it throughout the day. Choose wisely; do you choose to stay focused on the negative things about your life or do you choose to create a positive language to move you forward in life?

Chapter 6
Being Alert and Aware

Most people go through life doing whatever it takes to survive, going through each day doing the same things over and over again, unconscious to the reality of who they really are. They are stuck in the exaggerated stories of the past, living that past into their future in different ways, chasing dreams and goals that either are difficult to realise or never achieve them at all.

The reality today is that there are more and more people getting sick because of the stresses they are faced with each day, living in a rat race rushing back and forth just to keep up with that which they call life. Life seems to be throwing more and more challenges at us as we go through each year, and those challenges don't seem to be getting any easier.

This has resulted in human beings becoming disconnected from their true selves and realising that they have much more power to transform their lives than they think they have. The truth is that from the first day we were born, we have been programmed to be who we are today, it is only when we become fully aware of this reality, will we be able to actively transform our lives to becoming the powerful creative people that we really are.

Reconnecting to Yourself

You have already learnt that language is the first place of creation or transformation; however there is another aspect of your lives that you have to learn in-order to fully harness your true potential. You have to learn to reconnect with yourself from within. When you have this deeper self-connection; you are able to connect with others in a more powerful way, you will notice that you will start attracting people who can either guide you to the point where you need to be or help you along the way to achieving your goals and dreams.

Through this deep self-connection you will become more aware of your surroundings and other people, you will start to notice more things around you and will feel alert. I am not speaking of anything spiritual here, I am talking about a technique that gets you connected in a deep mental manner that will help you be alert to opportunities.

You may have heard the statement "Opportunity only knocks once" that in some sense may be true; however it is far from the truth. Most people never realise that opportunities actually come by almost every day, sometimes a number of times per day. It is only each opportunity that comes around once, and if we miss it, it is gone.

However when you become connected with yourself, in turn you will start to connect with others while becoming alert to things around you, you will start to notice all those opportunities all around you. With this awareness you will start to recognise how the words you are speaking is actually affecting you and will be able to create a new language that will move you forward.

You will notice that you are able to step into the unknown and it is not as scary as you may have thought it was. Through this self-awareness you will become more compassionate and less judgemental towards others allowing you to open your mind to be more focused on achieving your dreams.

Technique to Connect with Yourself

There is a simple technique that will help you become more connected with yourself, make you more aware of your surroundings and help you be more connected with other human beings. It will also help you with learning new things, in classrooms, seminars and so on, making you more alert to what you are learning and helping you retain the information for much longer. This will create a heightened sense of awareness and alertness which can increase your intuition and allowing you to make better decisions towards taking action.

The techniques that you are about to learn below are derived from various modalities which create mental alertness. Aspects of these techniques have been used for thousands of years in meditation, and later in hypno-therapy and NLP. They are powerful yet simple techniques that really increase your ability to be alert and aware.

These techniques should be practiced everyday if you really want to get connected to your creativity and intuition. Merely doing them once in a while is only going to increase your awareness for a couple of hours on the day you practice them, with daily practice you will notice a shift in how you notice things around you and will increase your awareness to numerous opportunities.

Initially it may take around ten minutes to practice these exercises, however within a week or two of daily practice you will notice that it can be done within five minutes. The better you get at it, the faster you will be able to get creative and achieve goals, overcome subconscious resistance with relative ease and feel more energised during the day.

Technique to become more Alert

This first technique can be done in five minutes and will help you be more alert, learn better and be fully aware of your surroundings. First find a quiet and comfortable place where you can sit. Find an object that you like which you can focus on, make sure that the object is not too small where you have to strain to stay focused on it. Place the object you are going to focus on a few feet in front of the chair you are sitting on, making sure you are several feet from the object so that if you stretch out your arm from where you are sitting, you are unable to touch the object.

Sit on the chair with your back straight, feet flat on the ground and palms of your hands resting comfortably on your lap, making sure that you do not cross your arms and legs. Once you are feeling comfortable in that seated position, focus your eyes on the object you had placed in front of you, keep focusing on the object until it is the only thing you are focused on. Do not allow your eyes to close. You want to keep your eyes open throughout this exercise.

Once you are fully focused on the object, keep your focus there but become aware of the left hand side of the room you are sitting in. Become aware of everything on the left side of the room, keep your eyes focused on the object, you just want to be aware of the left side of the room, allow your intuition to take over here.

Once you feel you are aware of the left side of the room and everything to the left, become aware of the right side of the room. Keeping focus on the object; allow yourself to become aware of everything on the right side of the room. Once you feel you are aware of everything to the left and right of the room, allow yourself to become aware of everything behind you, even if you have to imagine it, trust your intuition and allow yourself to be aware of what is behind you.

Now become aware of the other rooms in the house or apartment that you are sitting in. Become aware of the whole building and its surroundings even if you have to imagine it, again trust your intuition. Now allow yourself to become aware of the whole area or neighbourhood. Once you feel you are aware of the neighbourhood or area, allow yourself to become aware of the whole city. Once you are aware of the whole city, become aware of the whole country.

You don't have to get it one hundred percent right, just allow yourself to be aware of it intuitively or through your imagination, remember your eyes should still be open and focusing on the object in front of you. Now become aware of the whole continent that your country is located in. Next become aware of the whole earth. As you allow yourself to be aware of the whole earth, allow your mind to expand by becoming aware of outer space, expanding to be aware of all the other planets and the whole galaxy.

Now remain in this full awareness for a minute then allow your awareness to come back towards the planet earth. Be aware of the whole earth again, the continent your country is in then your country and back to your city. Now become aware of your area or neighbourhood again until you are back to the building you are in, all the rooms and now bring your awareness back into the room you are in. Take in a deep breath and relax your eyes from focusing on the object, let the breath out slowly through your mouth. Now notice just how alert you are feeling.

Performing the above exercise every morning will help you be alert throughout the day, helping you be aware of possible opportunities that could move you forward in your career or life. With constant practice you can do this exercise within five minutes. You can also use this exercise when you are attending lectures or seminars.

Sit in the lecture room or seminar hall and focus on something in front of you and complete the exercise as you have already learnt. This will open your mind to learning more and retaining information for much longer. You will also notice that you will be aware of everyone in the room or seminar hall, being able to notice the different colours people are wearing as well as feeling connected to yourself and the people around you. This creates the possibility of you being able to communicate with the people around you even if they are total strangers.

Over and above that, you will also feel connected to the person giving the lecture or conducting the seminar helping you to understand what they are teaching with more clarity. You can also use this technique at work to help you be more productive or find possible solutions to problems or conflicts within the work place.

There are numerous benefits to practicing this technique. The next technique will help you become more connected with yourself and assist you in becoming more intuitive and creative. It will also help you relax and be more calm when you are feeling stressed.

The following technique is very similar to the first technique you have already learnt, the difference is that you do this one with your eyes closed. This technique can also be done lying down if you wish and are not too tired or you will fall asleep.

Another Technique to Become more Alert

Sit comfortably in a chair with your back straight and your feet flat on the floor, place the palm of your hands on your lap in the most comfortable position for you. If you choose to lie down, make sure your body is straight with your arms straight at either side of your body, you can place your hands on the lower part of your abdominal area however do not cross your hands over each other.

Once you are sitting comfortably or lying comfortably, keep your eyes open at this point and take a deep breath. Take the breath in nice and deep then hold it for a few seconds. As you breathe out slowly through your mouth imagine your body is relaxing. Now take a second deep breath and hold it for a few seconds.

This time as you breathe out slowly through your mouth, imagine that the air is leaving through your feet as if to be removing all tension from your body and relaxing all your muscles. Finally take in a deep breath and as you breathe in deeply, allow your eyes to close gently. Hold your breath for a few seconds and as you breathe out slowly through your mouth, imagine the air is leaving your body through your feet and your body becomes completely relaxed.

Do not under estimate your imagination. Your body will respond to this. Now with your eyes closed, breathe in deeply through your nose and let it out slowly through your nose. Now breathe a little less deep but just deep enough in and out through your nose until you get a good breathing rhythm going. This will help your body to further relax. Keep focusing on your breathing rhythm until it feels as if you are completely relaxed and your mind is becoming clear.

Once you have a good breathing rhythm going and your body feels relaxed with your mind clear, with your eyes still closed draw your attention back to the room you are in. You don't have to worry about the details of the room or what is in or around the room, just allow your attention to be on the room in your mind's eye.

Now imagine that you are floating up towards the ceiling of the room. Imagine that you are floating through the ceiling moving higher and higher as if to be moving towards the sky. You become aware of the whole property that you have floated out of, then becoming aware of the area or neighbourhood where the property is located. You imagine that you are floating higher becoming aware of the whole city and as you imagine floating higher you become aware of the whole country.

You continue to imagine floating higher until you become aware of the continent where your country is located, finally floating into out of space where you are looking at the whole earth, being aware of the whole earth. You continue to imagine that you are floating higher and higher as if you are passing all the planets moving towards the end of the galaxy.

Continue imagining that you floating higher past the end of the galaxy and as you do you become aware of other galaxies and universes. Allow your imagination to flow here, imagine that you float up to a point where you standing on a large platform where you see openings to other universes as if you are in the centre point of all the universes.

It is quiet and empty and you feel safe and protected in this place. Allow yourself to be with this quiet and emptiness for a few moments. This increases awareness of self as well as helping you get connected with your intuition. If you find that your mind is wondering at this point, start breathing in deeply in and out of your nose until you have a rhythm going and then just focus on your breathing. Then allow yourself to go back to that quiet space of nothingness as if nothing exists, just you in this centre point of the universe.

After a few moments of being in this space of emptiness or nothingness, imagine that you are floating back down into the Milky Way galaxy, back past the planets towards earth. Imagine you are moving towards earth quite quickly now until you see the whole earth and are aware of it. You move into the atmosphere of earth becoming aware of the continent your country is based in.

You now become aware of your country and then your city, moving lower towards your area or neighbourhood. Moving down towards the property you live in, down into the building and back into the room. Now allow all this awareness to fade and go back to breathing deeply in and out of your nose until you have a good rhythm going. Now focus on this breathing for a minute or two. Then take in a really deep breath through your nose and let it out slowly through your mouth. Take in a second deep breath and as you let it out slowly through your mouth, open your eyes slowly.

Take in a third deep breath and let it out slowly through your mouth. You may feel a little sleepy here especially if this is the first time that you are doing this exercise; however notice how calm and relaxed you are feeling after performing this exercise. Even if you feel as if you have gained nothing from this exercise, I assure you that you have gained something. Your stress level will be way down and you will be feeling completely relaxed.

You will have to practice this exercise for a couple of months before you really start to get the full benefit of it. If you are patient and you are consistent with practicing this exercise, you will start to open yourself up to a higher degree of creativity and you will notice that you will start having some amazing ideas that could help you move forward in what you want to achieve.

You will also be aware of the language you are using regarding yourself and how you speak about achieving your goals, allowing you to be more creative with choosing the right language that will get you closer to achieving your goals or taking action on what it is you want to achieve. There are many benefits to practicing this exercise everyday which you will discover for yourself as you get more proficient with practicing this exercise.

Each person has their own unique experience with this exercise and it is there for them to discover it for themselves. Initially this exercise will take about ten to fifteen minutes to perform, however as you become more proficient it will only take about five to seven minutes to perform. Allow yourself to enjoy it, especially the calm and relaxed feeling it will give you and notice the difference it will make in your life after several months.

Technique to Seek Answers to Problems

The following technique is a very powerful technique for contemplation or seeking answers to problems or questions that have been on your mind for a long time. Although similar to the second technique in this chapter, it takes you to a deeper level of your subconscious mind, connecting you with your own higher intelligence.

This technique will further enhance your intuition and help you discover a higher inner power that could raise your intelligence level and ability to understand and comprehend on a different level. However chances are that you will have much more profound experiences. Each individual will have their own unique experience with this technique and therefore it is best for individuals to discover these experiences themselves than to discuss them here.

The technique is derived from the concept you have learnt from chapter one, the essence of you. If you have not grasped the concept of a new way of looking at creation that is okay, but I do suggest you read the chapter again. To get the full benefit of this technique it is important that you are able to put aside all your beliefs, whether spiritual, religious or cultural, anything that you believe the world to be, including everything you know right now.

The aim here is not to teach you a new form of spirituality or belief system, but to get you to a place where nothing exists on your mind so that you can open your mind to a new way of learning and empowering yourself. If you are struggling to understand this and cannot put aside your beliefs in spirituality, religion or culture for this moment then it is best to avoid this technique.

The only purpose of this technique is to connect you with your own higher power so that you can create a new language or thought that will guide you to achieving the life you want. The only way to do that is to create from a blank canvas so to speak, where there is nothing and you then creating something from nothing. This removes all blocks while you are creating your new language and goals so that you have more confidence and power to achieve those goals and dreams.

Once you are sitting in a comfortable place with your back straight, feet flat on the floor with your palms placed comfortably on your lap, make sure that your arms and feet are not crossed. You can also lie down making sure that your body is straight with your arms on either side of your body.

Take in a deep breath through your nose, as deep as possible so that you can feel your diaphragm move as well. Hold it for a few seconds then as you let your breath out through your mouth slowly imagine that all your muscles are relaxing with the release of the breath.

Take in a second deep breath and hold it for a few seconds. As you breathe out slowly through your mouth, this time imagine that the air is leaving through your feet and all the tension and stress in your body is leaving with the release of the breath.

Take in a third deep breath and hold it for a few seconds, as you release the breath slowly through the mouth, imagine again that the air is leaving through your feet taking with it all your thoughts, beliefs, stress and everything you currently know. Now take in a final deep breath and as you hold the breath for a few seconds allow your eyes to close gently.

As you release the breath slowly through your mouth, imagine once more that all stress, tension, thoughts and everything you think you know is leaving your body with that breath. Now draw your attention to your breathing and start breathing deeply in and out through your nose, not too deeply but just deep enough that it is comfortable for you. Keep breathing deeply in and out of your nose until you find that you have a good breathing rhythm.

Focus on this breathing rhythm until you feel that your mind feels clear. Now draw your attention to a new way of seeing creation. For this moment forget everything you know about creation and just allow yourself to experience creation in a different way to enhance the way you will achieve your goals and dreams.

Imagine that nothing exists; absolutely nothing exists only pure energy. In this moment there is no universe, there is nothing, just this pure energy. This energy is known as unity as it is the only thing that exists right now. This energy feels like it is totally unlimited as if it is the absolute oneness of this non-existent life.

From this pure energy; suddenly there is the essence otherwise known as thought, from this thought comes language known as power which creates the light or enlightenment.

Through enlightenment came knowledge and suddenly there is existence. The energy starts to form molecules, protons, electrons and atoms and we have the start of physical form but for the purpose of this creation we will call it spirit (here the word spirit does not refer to the soul or any such thing, merely the start of physical form).

This spirit expands into two forms, everything that is similar to each other known as the similitudes. The other is the attributes that which is unique to everything. From this point the physical form is created, the universe, the planets and everything that exists on planet earth.

Now go back to breathing deeply in and out of your nose until you get a rhythm going. Once you have a clear mind again, draw your attention to your body, your physical form. Now imagine that you are floating out of your body to become the spirit or energy form of you.

You don't have to physically feel that you are floating out of your body; you just have to imagine it or state it in words quietly in your mind if you are struggling to imagine or visualize this. As the energy form of you, imagine that you are floating up into the sky and that your energy is spreading out to cover the whole earth.

Imagine that your energy form continues to expand as if moving into out of space and engulfing the galaxy to the point where your energy form has spread throughout the Milky Way. Imagine that this energy form expands out of the universe and continues to expand engulfing all the other universes that may be out there. You don't have to see this with your mind's eye or visualize it; you just have to allow yourself to imagine that you are expanding your energy form in this way.

Now try to imagine that you are one with all the universes and everything within them. Once you are able to feel as if you are one with all the universes and everything within them, imagine that you are now the existence and knowledge. You then become the light, power and the essence, moving into that absolute oneness, the unlimited, and allow yourself to be in that state for a few minutes.

Now in that state of unlimited absolute oneness imagine that nothing exists. Allow yourself to be in that non-existence. When you are able to be in that space where nothing exists for a few minutes, you can now start stating what you want to achieve out of life. State it with confidence "I want to achieve" stating exactly what it is you really want. Then try and visualize or imagine the end result as if you have already achieved your goal, be with this vision for a few minutes. Then state "This must happen for me" and allow the image or sense of it to fade and go back to that space where nothing exists.

Stay in that space for a minute or two then imagine that you become the essence, power and light returning to knowledge and existence. Imagine that your energy form is moving out of the universes back into the Milky Way galaxy, moving back down towards earth. As you get to earth imagine that your energy form is getting smaller moving back towards the room you are in and back into your body.

Once you feel that you are back in your body, start breathing deeply again, in and out through your nose until you have a rhythm going. Breathe with that rhythm for a minute then take in a deep breath through your nose and slowly let it out of your mouth. Take in another deep breath and as you let it out of your mouth slowly, open your eyes slowly. Take in a final breath through your nose as deep as you can, hold it for a few seconds and then let it out of your mouth slowly. Do not get up from your position, especially after the first time of practicing this exercise, sit or lie there for a minute or two, then stretch out and move slowly out of the position you are sitting or lying in. You should be feeling very relaxed after this exercise.

This exercise should take about twenty or thirty minutes to perform, the more you practice it, the better your chances of creating a powerful language that will keep you in action toward achieving your goals and dreams. You don't have to believe in this as the form of creation if it goes against what you already believe. This is not meant to be another form of spirituality but to get you into that deep state of mind where you can really create whatever it is you dream of.

You will become more intuitive and alert to opportunities but most important you will create a deep self-connection that will help you believe in yourself more and more with each practice. Eventually there will be a deep self-acceptance that will help you become in tune with your own inner power.

If you find that you still cannot grasp the concept, there is no right or wrong here, performing this technique is only optional, the important thing is that you do what you feel is most comfortable to you. For those who choose to practice the above technique, in the beginning there is a chance that you will fall asleep while practicing or in the middle of the technique, do not get upset about it or feel you have achieved nothing, falling asleep in this exercise is a good thing especially for your body.

Be patient with this one and allow it to work for you naturally and eventually you will start to have some amazing and profound experiences. Remember you have choice and you can choose what you want to create or how you want to feel, allow yourself to have fun creating your new life and just enjoy the journey there and don't worry about the destination, things will take care of itself and you will get there. Avoid calculating how long or how much further you have to go to reach your goal, rather look back to where you started and notice how far you have come, that way you will be motivated to keep going. Enjoy the process and have fun with it on your journey of creating your new life.

Chapter 7
Power of Self-Love

For thousands of centuries human beings have been fighting wars, oppressing nations, fighting to be the most powerful. There's greed and a hunger to have more at the cost of the lives of others. Human beings have been the oppressors, and then there is the oppressed, facing poverty and hunger. The world has had to deal with all of this including murder, rape, theft, racism and so much more until this very day.

The reality is that the majority of people have hopes for peace throughout the world. There are millions of people in this world from different walks of life, different religions or spiritual groups, even organizations for humanity, who are constantly working or praying to achieve world peace, alleviate world hunger and poverty, hoping to create an equal and peaceful society for all to live in harmony.

The truth is that no matter how much people pray or strive to achieve this, it is plain to see in this day and age that clearly we are nowhere near achieving that. This does not mean that there is anything wrong with praying

113

or religions or other spiritual groups. The fact of the matter is that with everything that religious and spiritual groups including humanity organizations do, there will always be wars, power hungry groups, greed, oppressors and oppressed, poverty and hunger, theft, murder and rape, even more for centuries to come.

Over and above all of that we see people turning to other forms of destruction just to escape the current reality. We see people destroying their lives through substance or alcohol abuse trying to escape their current reality because they see no way out of it. At the same time they are destroying their own lives they are creating a breakdown in the lives of the people around them.

People are constantly searching for answers, escapes and the rush just to find something exciting. The only thing they seem to find is more challenges and a stronger disconnect from themselves. That dream of world peace and harmony may never be realised because there is one vital element that human beings are missing.

Even though there are people aware of this missing vital element, the reality is that the majority of human beings resist it. They struggle to accept it and deal with what needs to be dealt with. It is the hardest thing for human beings to do, which is really deal with themselves and take responsibility.

Most people are too busy trying to fix what is wrong in the world or wanting to fix others rather than transforming themselves. The truth is that the only way to change the world is to change ourselves. That vital element that people resist is the power of self-love and self-forgiveness, which also includes gratitude.

Gratitude

Many authors and coaches always speak of gratitude, some have even written whole chapters and books about the power of gratitude. There is probably not much I could add to what is already available out there on gratitude. The practice of gratitude has a number of benefits that help you create emotions and powerful positive language that makes personal transformation a little easier. Gratitude triggers emotions of joy allowing you to feel positive about yourself. When you practice gratitude, you release emotions of appreciation which creates the feeling of having much more than you really have.

This trains your subconscious mind to associate with that feeling of joy which helps you appreciate what you have now and prolongs the feeling of enjoyment so that when you have something new in your life, you will really enjoy it for longer periods of time rather than it just being a novelty where the enjoyment of it fades within a few days.

The other benefit is that you start to attract more positive things in your life whether it is material objects or people that will keep you inspired to achieve your goals. This state of joy becomes a habit that helps you keep creating and drives your passion to achieve more in the areas that you love.

To train yourself to be in that constant state of joy and gratitude, you can start by being grateful for three to five things that you have in your life right now, state each day three or five things that you are grateful for. This also helps to humble you and prevent you from being compulsive or getting into the state of greed. Most importantly, gratitude helps you create a positive language that in turn will lead you to creating a positive language about yourself.

It is through this self-acceptance will your positive transformation be much easier. Through your positive language about yourself; you will be more willing to deal with all those negative issues that have been holding you back for so long.

This does not mean that it is just going to transform by magic, you still have to deal with those negatives however it will be much easier as there will be less resistance from the subconscious mind especially when you are able to create happiness and those feelings of joy no matter what the circumstances.

With less resistance there will be more self-transformation which will also help in creating more patients in dealing with your issues or with other people. You will also find that you will become less judgemental about situations and will start looking at those issues objectively rather than subjectively.

In short gratitude will train you to choose happiness first over and above everything else, remember in earlier chapters, almost every coach says that you have to first learn to be happy before you can have what you want because it is not the things or other people that make you happy, only you can choose to be happy, gratitude creates those emotions and language that will help you get there faster.

Although gratitude is powerful and there are a number of benefits to practicing gratitude, it does not clear out the past that we subconsciously hold on to, for that we have to learn the art of forgiveness. When we are able to completely clear our attachments to the past, we open up a space where we can create the future we want rather than living into the future based on our past.

116

Forgiveness

Forgiveness is not easy to achieve at first, especially when there has been traumatic situations involved in the past. Forgiveness does not mean that those who caused the traumatic situations are suddenly let off the hook but it is about you as the individual cutting your ties and freeing yourself.

When you hold on to something especially when there is hurt involved, even if the person or persons' who caused the hurt are no longer in your life physically, the emotional and mental attachment keeps you attached to them. This means they will never be out of your life and it will be very difficult for you to transform yourself because you not only will lack in trust of others but you will have little self-trust. This will cause you to have little self-esteem and self-belief.

Forgiveness allows you to detach from all of that and it will free you mentally and physically from the chains that are holding you back, keeping you blocked from your own true power. For most people it is not going to be easy at first to forgive and move on, it is a practice you really have to work at.

There will be times where you think you may have forgiven someone but there could be very strong emotional attachments that have held you back from fully forgiving, it will rear its ugly head from time to time. That is why forgiveness is an art that you have to learn and keep practicing.

The more you practice the art of forgiveness, the more you clear out your past to create a whole new bright and beautiful future. Through sincere forgiveness you will notice a difference in your health as well, not only will you feel healthier, you will feel lighter and even your appearance will look better. That lightness can be seen in your face and you will be surprised of the compliments you will start receiving.

Once you are able to fully practice the art of forgiveness, you start to realise that you can resolve conflict caused in the present much more quickly and easily. This will clear your path to creating and achieving much more than you have dreamt possible.

With the art of forgiveness comes another difficult task and that is asking for forgiveness. Sometimes it is so difficult to ask for that forgiveness especially when you totally believe that it was not your fault. When it comes to asking for forgiveness, it really does not matter who was right or wrong, asking for forgiveness has the same effect as forgiving, it allows you to free yourself from the attachments you have with the other person.

Saying I am sorry whether you were right or wrong actually gives you power, you get to let go of the conflict even if the other person does not forgive you. You get to free yourself from them and release all those negative emotions that they choose to stay with. However if they do not forgive you, it is important that you learn to forgive yourself.

Forgiving others or asking for forgiveness does not mean that you have to be friends or keep company with the other person; it is about you completely freeing yourself from them. Asking and giving forgiveness face to face is very powerful, however it can also be done on the phone or in meditation if it is not possible to do it in person.

You will have to check within yourself from time to time to see if you have really forgiven others by noticing whether emotions of anger or bitterness comes up when you think of them. If no such emotions come up when you think of them, you are free and will be able to go forth and start enjoying your life.

This freedom will even help you create more positive language about yourself that will really increase your ability to believe in yourself to create the life you want. Also equally important is that you have to learn to forgive yourself for all the hurt you may have caused and release all the guilt that you are carrying. You will also have to forgive yourself for carrying that guilt.

Furthermore you will have to forgive yourself for all the negative things that you have said about yourself throughout the years. This also allows you to free yourself from that burden of the past and let go of the negative way you saw yourself for all those years. As you get better at practicing this self-forgiveness you will notice that it will get easier to forgive others and also ask for forgiveness with sincerity.

You will start to feel lighter and lighter and don't be surprised if miracles start popping up in front of you on a regular basis. You will even look better and people will be attracted to your positive energy without you even having to say a word to them. Your life will transform in ways that you have never dreamed possible.

Self-Love

Another difficult task for most people to perform is the task of self-love. Self-love is the most powerful of all transformations that human beings will ever experience. I am not talking about the narcissist self-consumed type of love where you think you the most important thing in the world and others are beneath you, I am speaking of a deep unconditional self-love that radiates from the depths of your heart.

This self-love can only fully be obtained with the practice of forgiveness. When you are able to love yourself from your heart unconditionally, no matter what you look like or what your current circumstances may be, you open yourself up to a transformation that is more powerful than anything you have ever experienced.

Through this self-love the world around you will transform for you. You will not judge others or even put others down bringing you a sense of peace that nobody or nothing in this universe can give you. When you are at peace and have peace in your heart, everything around you becomes peaceful. As strange as this may sound, whether you believe it or not, it will be difficult to grasp until you have the experience of it yourself.

The secret to life is that you do not have to change the world, when you change yourself from within, the whole world will transform to accommodate you. Those who have fully experienced this self-love can never fully express in words the profound experiences that they have every day of their life. Each individual will have their own unique experience and each one of those experiences will truly be profound.

When you are in this state of unconditional self-love, that love will radiate out of your heart and people around you will feel this amazing energy. They will be drawn to you because of the amazing energy you radiate but also due to your ability to be non-judgemental and at peace. There will be very little room for conflict in your life.

When you combine gratitude, forgiveness and self-love into your way of being, you will experience immense power that will have you living a life of what we mortals would call magic and adventure. When I talk of gratitude, unconditional forgiveness and unconditional self-love, I am not speaking from a place of spiritual or religious teachings.

Each individual will find their own calling or already have their own calling right now in their practices of religion or spirituality. Some may not like what is being said here, however whether you like it or not, it is the absolute truth, even an atheist can have those profound experiences and miracles through gratitude, forgiveness and self-love like everyone else.

Believing in self-love, unconditional forgiveness and gratitude does not have to be a spiritual practice but a choice. Through this choice you can create an abundant life that you had never dreamt of before, you will experience abundance in absolutely every aspect of your life and those around you will benefit from that abundance.

However getting to that point is not going to be easy, only if you are willing to do what it takes will you be able to achieve it. This will require patience and persistence on your part no matter how difficult it may seem. You will face a lot of resistance on this journey of unconditional self-love but the persistence and sacrifice is really worth the effort.

How long it takes to get there is really up to you, it will all depend on how long you take to get started and how persistent you are on practicing it every day. There will be times when you feel you want to give up, that is your resistance talking and the negative voices in your head, all you have to do is change your language and say "I deeply and completely love myself" or "I deeply and completely love and accept myself". It all starts with the words that you are willing to say to yourself.

Self-love starts with you standing in front of the mirror each day for at least two or three minutes, stating "I love you and I appreciate you". As you start to accept those words and start feeling the emotions of those words, the emotions of love, you can extend the time to five minutes and state "I love and appreciate you unconditionally".

Another powerful way to get to that state of self-love is to give yourself fifteen minutes a day to sit in a quiet place and go into a meditative state and say the words "I am love", then use it throughout the day as an affirmation. To get into the meditative state is very simple; you don't have to be in any specific position. All you have to do is find a quiet and comfortable spot to sit or lie in. Once you are comfortable, take in a deep breath through your nose and hold it for a few seconds then let it out of your mouth slowly.

Repeat this another two times and on your third breath in, close your eyes gently. After you release your third breath and your eyes are closed, start breathing gently and deeply in and out of your nose until you find you have a rhythm going with your breath. Focus on this breathing for a few minutes until you feel your mind is clear.

Once you feel clear and your breathing is a rhythmic gentle deep breathing, as you breathe out, state in your mind "I am" and as you breathe in, state in your mind "love". This will take some practice because in the beginning it is easy to get confused and state "I am" as you breathe in and "love" as you breathe out. The aim is to feel that love or self-love that is why you breathe out "I am" and breathe in "love".

Once you have this right, practice it each day for fifteen minutes with patience and no expectations. When you ready to leave the meditative state, all you have to do is take in a deep breath through your nose and breathe out slowly through your mouth three times, opening your eyes as you release your breath slowly on the second breath out of your mouth. You can now go about your day as normal.

If you choose to use "I am love" as an affirmation, you can further enhance it by breathing deeply in and out of your nose even if you are not going to go into the meditative state. You can do this breathing any time, while walking, working or busy with whatever it is you doing. All you have to remember is that as you breathe out state in your mind "I am" and as you breathe in state in your mind "love". The breathing rhythm will keep you calm and you will start to feel the benefits of that self-love fairly quickly.

Once again I state clearly this is not just from spiritual teachings, it is for everyone who chooses to transform their life no matter what their religious, spiritual or cultural practices are. It does not matter whether you are male or female, your sexual orientation or your background and education; it will have the same effect and power for everyone equally.

Many people talk about finding their purpose, some search for years and others may discover it within a short while, whatever your purpose, the first purpose in life is that deep unconditional self-love. When you are able to find that no matter whom you are, you will find your true purpose within minutes and you will transform your life into abundance, fun and adventure.

You will find true peace and be at peace with everything and everyone. You will find your passion and succeed every time with it no matter what it is you choose to do. You will find that life actually gets easier and you will have a sense of calmness and protectiveness. You will notice that you will always be in the right place at the right time and will always achieve what you want to achieve.

The truth is, whether you choose to believe it or not, whether you choose to practice it or not, the purpose of life is unconditional self-love no matter who you are. This is the missing element in life; until each individual person chooses to recognise this and accept this, then bring that deep unconditional self-love into their hearts, only then will we probably see the peace and harmony on earth that so many people dream about. It takes loving you to create the life you really want nothing is more powerful than that.

Chapter 8
Disconnecting from Emotional Attachments

When you have experiences through events that have occurred in your life, whether it be positive or negative experiences from those events, emotions associated with those events are triggered. Positive and negative emotions can also be triggered through belief and value systems, whether those beliefs and values were created from your own perspective or through the influence of your parents, guardians, teachers, religion and culture.

The way you see and perceive yourself also triggers associated negative or positive emotions. These emotions are stored as memory on the subconscious mind, which are later triggered and released into the body when you think of specific events of the past, when something does not conform to your belief and value systems or when you have negative thoughts of yourself.

It is the negative emotions associated with all of that, which becomes the attachments or blocks that create the obstacles that stand in your way of achieving your goals and dreams. When you are able to detach from those negative emotional attachments, it becomes easier to resolve past issues and overcome the obstacles that hold you back.

An event refers to everything that has occurred in your life, from the day you were born to the present day. These events become stored memories and have emotions attached to them, such as happiness, joy, excitement, sadness, trauma and even love and hate.

An event can be something as simple as a petty argument with a friend or parent, to something traumatic such as a car accident and so on. When you are faced with similar situations to past events, or hear stories of events that relate to some of your past events, if those events were not positive in your life, negative emotions attached to those events would be triggered even though you are in a different time and place or even just hearing or thinking about those events.

For example, if a person has been chased or bitten by a dog, every time after that event, the negative emotions of those events are triggered whenever the person sees or hears a dog bark. Similarly when you are told "No" for a request you made, emotions attached to that "No" are triggered whenever you have to make a request to the same person or even others.

Maybe you failed at achieving a goal or something big like losing a business, every time you try and start a new big project, that feeling of failure is triggered, causing you to struggle to get started or achieve your goal. It does not matter what the past memories are, it is the emotional attachment in your present time that is associated with that past memory which causes you to either back off from moving forward, fail to complete a goal, procrastinate or even repeat the same mistakes over and over again. The key to resolving problems, having breakthroughs, breaking out of your comfort zones, is emotional detachment.

Emotional detachment does not mean that you become an emotionless person; it is the detachment to those triggered emotions that causes all the blocks and obstacles in your life. Detaching emotionally will vary from person to person depending on how strong the emotional attachments are. Therefore some people may need to work with a coach or therapist while others may be able to do it themselves from what they learn here.

There is no right or wrong way whether you need help or can do it yourself. If you are unable to do it yourself, it does not make you a bad or useless person in anyway, it merely means that the emotion is too strong and needs to be broken down in stages with the help of a guide.

Remember that positive and negative emotions cannot exist in the same place at the same time, in this case in your body and thoughts. It is very simple to switch negative emotions into positive ones within minutes, this can be done by just shifting your thoughts, listening to music that makes you happy, or doing something that will make you laugh. There is a saying, laughter is the best medicine, therefore try and laugh a little more everyday even if you have to trigger that laughter yourself.

There are three techniques that I like to use to detach from the negative emotions that creep up from time to time when trying to achieve specific goals. These are fairly simple techniques which I use regularly on myself or in my practice. They literally detach those negative emotions within minutes and help to transform you into feeling powerful and motivated.

However it is important to note that if there are strong negative emotions caused from trauma in the past or negative emotions associated with depression or psychological issues, these techniques will not work. Therefore it is important that anyone struggling with emotional issues reoccurring from traumatic or psychological situations seek the assistants or help of trained or licenced councillors before using these techniques on themselves.

If you find that these techniques are not working as well as you would like it to, you may want to seek the assistants of either a hypnotherapist, NLP practitioner or life coach, to help break down those negative attachments step by step. It is also important to note that these techniques will not resolve current or past problems and situations automatically; they merely break through the negative emotions that hold you back from dealing with problems or achieving goals in a positive way.

Once the emotional attachment or negative emotion has disappeared it then becomes easier to focus on solutions and find resolutions to current or existing problems. It also helps you generate positive emotions that can help you become more creative.

When using these techniques, avoid thinking of the problem or cause of the negative emotion in detail. The aim is to get through or past the negative emotion as quickly as possible. These techniques should not take longer than a maximum of ten to fifteen minutes to complete.

If you find that you are dealing with the same negative emotion for longer than fifteen minutes, it could probably be that you are getting too focused on the event that triggered those negative feelings, stop all your thoughts and then refocus on the technique again. Remember these are simple techniques to break through the negative emotions and to transform them into positive ones; they are not solutions to past or present problems.

This first technique is very simple yet effective. Derived from NLP, it will help you deal with negative emotions that suddenly come up or make you feel stuck in any given moment. This technique will not resolve your issue but will help you disconnect from it emotionally helping you look at the problem without any emotional attachments, freeing you up mentally to resolve whatever issue you may be dealing with in that moment. This technique should take at least five minutes or less to perform depending on the strength of the negative emotions.

Dealing with Negative Emotions

Find a comfortable chair to sit in, sit up straight with your head and eyes faced straight forward. Your body or head must not move while performing this exercise. Now with your eyes straight; move your eyeballs downward as if to look at the floor, while keeping your head faced straight ahead.

While your eyes are facing down; think of a problem or situation that may be affecting you emotionally in this moment, avoid thinking or getting bogged down in the detail of the problem or situation. Once you know the problem and can feel the emotion of it, think of a number between zero and ten. Zero is no emotion at all and ten is worse or high negative feeling.

Do not sit and think of a number just let the first number that pops in your head be the number you feel toward the negative emotion. Once you have the number, bring the eyes up as if to look up at the ceiling. Do not think of the negative emotion at this point, just look up at the ceiling with your eyes making sure that your head is still facing straight ahead.

Now that your eyes are facing up, count to fifteen quietly in your mind as fast as you can and then allow yourself to smile. Give yourself the biggest smile that you can give, the smile is for you so just allow that smile to be there. After a few seconds, count to fifteen as fast as you can again and then smile the biggest smile you can give yourself. After a few seconds of smiling; count to fifteen once more as fast as you can in your mind and then smile again.

After you have given yourself a big smile for the third time, hold that smile for a few seconds and then bring your eyes down to look at the floor again, remember to keep the head straight ahead. Think of the negative emotion again and give it the first number that pops into your head, the number should be lower now, for example it should have come down from an eight to a five.

If the number is zero then you have cleared all the emotions attached to that negative situation. If the number is still not zero, keep practicing the above exercise by looking up again, counting to fifteen and smiling, repeat this until you find that number has come down to zero. Once it is at zero you will feel a lot better, you can use this for as many negative emotions that pop up at any time of the day. You will feel good about yourself and will be able to think of ways to resolve problems from a more positive perspective.

A Second Technique

The second technique is just as simple but will require that you do it standing up. It is great for transforming your emotions and leaving you feeling empowered and happy. It will require that you have some patience and it should take you around five to ten minutes to perform, you will need to use your imagination a little for this one.

This technique will not resolve the negative situation automatically even though it may feel like it immediately after performing it, however it will leave you empowered to deal with the situation and resolve it. Do not underestimate the simplicity of this technique; you will notice an immediate difference in your emotions.

Find a quiet space where you can practice this technique and make sure that you have an empty space of at least three or four feet in front of you. Stand up straight and think of the negative situation that is currently bothering you, you can also choose a situation from the past that is still triggering negative emotions.

Get a feel of those negative emotions, remember do not think of the details of the situation or get caught up in how it all started, just think of the situation and let the negative emotions associated with that situation come up. Give it a number between zero and ten like in the first technique, zero being no feeling at all and ten being the worst.

Do not waste time thinking of a number, go with the first number that pops in your head. Once you have a number, look out on to the floor in the space in front of you. Imagine that in this empty space in front of you there is a circle that is big enough for you to stand in. It does not have to be a circle; it can also be a square, a small platform or a transparent cubicle.

Choose whatever you like and give it a colour that you love the most. For the purpose of this discussion we will use the imaginary platform. With your right foot take a big step onto the imaginary platform. While standing on the platform, you can close your eyes at this point if you wish, think of the first time you really felt happy, one of the happiest time of your life. Once you have called up that happy time, allow yourself to really feel that happy feelings. Once you feel those happy feelings, think of the second time you were most happy. Get in touch with those happy feelings and really call them up and feel them.

Now think of the third time you were most happy and really call up all those feelings of happiness. Now that you are feeling this happiness, think of the first time you felt really empowered. Call up those empowering feelings and really get in tune with them and feel them. Now think of a second time you felt really empowered and call up those feelings of empowerment and really feel them.

Finally think of the third time you felt empowered and call up and feel those feelings of empowerment. Now just feel those feelings of happiness and empowerment. Once you can really feel happy and empowered, with your left foot step backwards off the imaginary platform.

Call up the negative situation you originally called up and take note if there are any negative emotions. If there are negative emotions still there, give it a number; the first number that pops in your head. You will notice that the number is lower than the original number you originally had.

Step back onto that imaginary platform with your right foot and repeat the process, calling up the three times when you were most happy and the three times when you felt most empowered and really get in touch with those feelings. Then step backwards off the platform with your left foot. Call up the negative emotion again and give it a number, if it is still not at zero repeat the process until you get to zero.

If the negative emotion is at zero, step back onto the imaginary platform with your right foot, then call up all those happy and empowered feelings, you just have to call up and feel happy and empowered you don't have to think of the three times you were happy and empowered.

Now step off the platform with your right foot moving forward in front of you. When you are at zero and you go back onto the platform you step off in front of you as you are moving forward in life. From this moment if the negative emotions of the situation you have just dealt with come up again, all you have to do is imagine the imaginary platform, maybe the circle or square if you chose that, and step into it and just call up those happy and empowered emotions.

You can also imagine stepping into the circle, square or imaginary platform which ever one you chose at any time even if you are not feeling negative. You can just step into it and call up feelings of happiness or empowerment, even feelings of times when you felt most powerful. You can do this if you just want to feel powerful and achieve tasks with positive energy. After you have created this imaginary circle, square or platform in your favourite colour, you can imagine yourself in it at any time you want to feel empowered and you can also imagine that you are in it even while sitting in your chair at your desk at work.

This will help you trigger empowering emotions that will help you resolve most situations fairly easily and also help you overcome any negative emotions you may have if you had failed at achieving your goals. You can use this along with your new positive language to really get ahead at achieving your goals and dreams.

A Third Technique

The third technique requires the use of imagination and some visualization, it helps you to look at events that occurred in the past which still trigger negative emotions today from an objective perspective rather than the subjective perspective you currently have of that past event.

The objective with this technique is to first disconnect the emotional attachments to the event then to look at the event objectively, identifying what you can learn from it or what positive messages can you take from that event. At first give yourself at least ten minutes per event you deal with, once you become proficient at practicing this, you will be able to do it in five minutes.

Find a quiet place where you can practice this technique without being disturbed. You will need to stand for this one. Take in a deep breath through your nose and let it out slowly through your mouth to get yourself relaxed. Repeat this two more times and just be relaxed. You can close your eyes if you need to. Think of an event that occurred in the recent past or longer if you wish, which still triggers negative emotions to this day.

If the event is a traumatic event, please work with a trained coach who can assist you through the process. The technique here is for those who can use it on their own. Once you have chosen the event you want to work on, take note of the negative emotion and give it a number from zero to ten. Zero being no feeling at all and ten being the worst. Once you have the number of the intensity of the emotion, stand and look at the empty space of floor in front of you.

Imagine that you are on a top floor and looking down through the floor as if to look into a room below your floor. Imagine that the event you are working on is happening in that room. As you watch the event play through in that room below you, imagine that you start floating up and the images of the event start getting smaller and smaller until you cannot see the event at all, only a tiny dot on the floor.

Now that you are looking down on that event as a tiny dot, take note of the negative emotion toward that event and give it the first number that pops in your head. That number should be lower now, for example when you first took note of the negative emotion, if it was nine, it should have come down to six. If the number is not at zero, float back down to the point where you were looking at the event from above and then float back up again until you see the event as just a dot on the floor.

Take note of the negative emotion and give it the first number that pops in your head. If the number has not come down to zero, float back down again to the event and back up until you only see a dot on the floor, repeat the process until you get to zero.

Once the negative emotion has come down to zero, which means there is no emotion attached to the event at all, float back down to the event but this time imagine that you are floating down right into the event as if you are there again. If the negative emotions start to rise, give it the first number that pops in your head and then float back up again until you only see a dot on the floor.

Generally the emotion will go back to zero when you float up again. Now float right back down into the event as if you are in that event, if the negative emotion rises again, repeat the process until you can imagine yourself being right in the event with no negative emotion. Once you have no negative emotion toward the event, float up just high enough as to be looking down at the event as if it is in a room just below you.

Now look at the event as if you are an outsider looking in and see what you can learn from that event. Usually at this point you should be able to see or come up with resolutions for the problems caused by that event. If you are not able to come up with resolutions, don't worry about it, look into the event again and ask yourself what positive messages you can take from this event, usually at this point you will find positive things to learn from that event. Now imagine you floating up again until the event is just a dot on the floor below you. Take in a deep breath and release the air slowly, open your eyes if they were closed, you are now complete with this event.

You can test whether you have completely let go of the negative emotions and events that have affected you by imagining you are right there in the event again, however to test if you have completely let go, do not do it immediately after you have practiced the techniques above. Wait several hours or preferably twenty four hours.

Imagine that you are right in that event again, remember not to get caught up in the details or cast blame on who started it. All you do is imagine that you are in that event again and take note if any negative emotions arise. If negative emotions do rise again, stop imagining the event and repeat the technique you used the day before to release the negative emotions by repeating the process of those respective techniques.

Sometimes you may have to repeat the process several times over depending on how strong the negative emotions were. The longer you have been holding on to those negative emotions, you may need to practice the techniques a number of times to completely let it go. This does not mean that there is something wrong with you; it is only that you are strongly attached to that past. Try and be kind to yourself and practice having patience with resolving that past, you want to experience the lightness of letting go and having the space to fully focus on achieving your dreams.

Being kind to you also means being able to forgive yourself for holding on to the negative emotions for so long, as well as forgiving all those who were involved. You will be amazed at how your life will transform once you have completely let go of all those negatives that have been holding you back for so long.

You know that your habits and behaviours are programmed into you from events of the past, including the environment where you grew up. These are all programmed into your subconscious mind and it literally controls the way you do things in the world as you try to move forward in life.

The most important part of all of that are the words that you speak to yourself. Now that you are aware that internal language affects the way you perform, all you have to do is get rid of those exaggerated stories and conversations going on in your head. Start seeing things for what they really are and not from perception.

Use your power of language to start transforming yourself; you do have all the necessary tools to create the words and language that will transform your life. There is nothing more powerful than you creating your own positive language and training yourself to be aware of it.

You have added tools and have learnt that you can quickly change the way you feel, from negative to positive, within minutes. However the important thing to remember is that you have to learn the art of forgiveness no matter how difficult it may be and add gratitude as well as self-love to make that transformation more powerful.

The more you use powerful and kind words on yourself the more confident you will feel to take action. Taking action is easy if you stop thinking and just go ahead and try to take the actions when you have declared exactly what you want. Try not to take life so seriously and really allow yourself to have fun with following your passion and being the success you deserve to be.

The reality is that it is not about how much or what you can achieve but about you learning to love yourself first and being happy now, allowing yourself to see yourself as the success that you are before it actually happens and not getting caught up in what is going on around you. Self-development and transformation is not going to be easy, it is very difficult when it comes to dealing with you, the important thing is to be persistent with patience and allow it to happen naturally.

It is not about what others think or say but what it is that you really want. You now have the tools to recognise where or why you have blocks and obstacles, the choice is in your hands whether you are going to practice it or not. Even though this journey may not be easy, you can still have fun doing it and really enjoy every moment on the road to achieving your dreams.

Chapter 9
Visualization: A
Subconscious Language

The power of visualization is not a new concept, it has been used for centuries and is one of the most talked about technique in achieving goals for more than sixty years. Every coach whether it be in the field of self-development, sports or the arts, talk about visualization as a powerful tool to getting your goals achieved.

It has brought about tremendous results for some people, while others find that they are still struggling to get things right. There are also those who cannot visualize and most of them end up giving up their goal because of it. However for those that struggle to visualize their goal, does not mean they have to see it in their mind.

Imagination and intuition will help in the same way. For example everyone knows what an apple looks and tastes like, using your imagination you can close your eyes and get a sense of the apple, remembering its scent and taste, which is like feeling the apple in your mind as opposed to seeing it.

There are a number of techniques that non visual people can use to get around the inability to visualize. However in the same way, you can train your mind to visualize to a certain extent provided you are willing to do the exercises and be patient to allow the visuals to come naturally.

I was one of those people who could not visualize, yet with practice and over time I am now able to visualize and when I cannot see the images in my mind, I can get a strong sense of it, thus feeling it as if through my other senses rather than seeing it. It usually has the same effect as being able to visualize vividly and clearly. If you are non-visual, some of the information here will help you to develop a greater sense on the mind that will be a powerful tool for achieving goals.

For hundreds of years and to this current day, the subconscious mind has and still is one of the biggest areas of study in the area of humanity. Regularly scientists, doctors, psychologists and hypnotherapists are discovering new attributes of the subconscious mind.

I believe that we as human beings have only scratched the surface of just how powerful the inner workings of the subconscious mind really are. I can't help wonder if the subconscious mind is one of the most powerful attributes available to human kind that exists within the context of the universe.

I have found through my practice of working with others, if you train the mind first, the body will automatically follow. This means that the subconscious mind creates all the habits and behaviours necessary for transformation of the way we take action in achieving our goals.

When you are able to access the inner depths of your subconscious mind, commonly known as the theta level, you can create images, words and context sentences that will help you develop attitudes and behaviours that make it easier to achieve your goals and dreams. This may sound complex and quite technical to do, but in reality it is very simple but it is having the discipline and motivation to perform the exercises on a daily basis that makes it feel difficult to perform.

The other aspect that makes it feel difficult to achieve your dreams, are the subconscious resistance that will always take place. To overcome this resistance, you have to stay disciplined, persistent, focused and consistent on your goal. You don't have to spend hours a day practicing exercises or visualising your goals, once you know how to access your subconscious mind directly, you can perform those exercises for five to ten minutes two or three times a day.

As you will learn and discover that it is really that simple, it is the context of complexity in which most people grow up that makes it difficult when learning this new simple concept. Sometimes the most simple of techniques are the most powerful solutions and tools to positive and empowering transformation.

One of the main attributes of the subconscious mind is that it cannot distinguish between reality and fantasy. What we as human beings identify or know as fantasy on the conscious level, can be perceived as real on the subconscious level. For example when you watch a movie, if it is a horror movie, you consciously know that it is only a movie and the characters in the movie are actors who are acting out the various scenes.

Basically you know on the level of the conscious mind that what you are watching is not real, on the other hand though, on the subconscious mind it feels and looks very real, thus the subconscious mind will trigger the emotions and adrenalins related to fear, getting your body ready for flight or fight situations. The same for sad scenes, you know it's just a movie or acting yet you tear up or feel sad, happy if it is happy or exciting scenes, a level of excitement if it is an action scene.

Whatever you may be watching whether it is on a cinema screen or television, the subconscious mind sees this fantasy as real and triggers emotions related to the scenes you are watching. What this really means is that when you sit in front of the television or at the cinema, while watching those movies, you go into a state of hypnosis. There are differing states, levels and forms of hypnosis and watching television or movies on any type or size of screen triggers a state of hypnosis.

The next time you watch a movie or listen to people talk about a movie or their favourite television show or soap opera, notice how you talk about the movie, chances are you will be describing scenes in the movie as if they happened in real life.

Notice people who speak about their favourite dramas and soap operas on television, notice how they speak of these shows as if it were real problems of people in their own lives. They are oblivious to the fact that they are speaking of something that is a fairy tale or fantasy.

Take it another step forward especially if you are hooked to soap operas, notice how many real life soap operas are going on around you, with your own family, colleagues and friends. Become aware of all of this and you will be surprised just how many real life soap operas exist in your life, all attracted to you from merely watching fantasy.

This does not mean that what you watch is going to happen in your life in the exact same way, there will be subtle real life issues that simulate the constantly observed fantasy. Put in another way, most people who watch violent movies are not suddenly going to become violent; in reality they probably never do become violent.

However they will be attracted to violence in some subtle way, they will regularly either hear stories of people who have experienced violence in their life in some way or they will experience an armed robbery, or constantly hear about violence in some part of the world. The attraction to violence will happen in different forms and not necessarily mean the individual will go out and purposefully look for varying forms of violence. In short, the fantasy you regularly watch is attracted into your life in subtle similarities of varying forms or levels.

Knowing that the subconscious mind cannot distinguish between reality and fantasy allows you the opportunity to take advantage of a powerful tool that can get you very close to achieving as many goals as you desire. Bear in mind that the fantasy that you dream up onto your subconscious mind, is not going to happen one hundred percent exact in the real world.

In reality you will come close to your fantasy, however it is not just going to fall out of the sky in the way you dream it, you will have to take action when opportunities arise, as well as being alert to those opportunities. There will be times where the opportunities will be staring you straight in the face but you will dismiss it for varying reasons, this does not mean those opportunities will not show up again, you will have to be alert enough to recognise them, thus meaning that achieving your goals will take a little longer than anticipated.

There are a number of ways to take advantage of the area of subconscious mind that cannot distinguish between reality and fantasy; this will require some focus, discipline and regular practice on your part to really make this powerful tool work for you. It will feel hard initially, especially during subconscious resistance, however with deep focus and persistence you can really make things happen for you faster and easier.

The trick is to find the correct time and place for you, where you can have five or ten minutes to place these goals onto the alpha or theta level of the subconscious mind. If you can get to the theta level of mind, you stand a stronger chance of creating the habits, behaviours and attitudes that will make it easier and fun to achieve your goals quickly.

Due to the subconscious mind not being able to distinguish between reality and fantasy, visualisation can be used as a positive language on the subconscious. It is the vision and words that you create around what you visualize that makes it stronger or weaker.

The Vision Board

The first form of visualization is the vision board. This is nothing new and has been around for a long time. To make the vision board really work for you, especially at a faster pace, is to put it up in a place where it is the first thing you see in the morning when you wake up and the last thing you see at night when you go to sleep.

This does not mean that if you have a vision board in your office or another place it will not work, vision boards work as long as you are visualising the pictures you put on it every day. Having the vision board in your bedroom placed in a position where it is the first and last thing you see every day, allows you to see those images on the theta level where it becomes imaged directly onto your subconscious mind.

When you go to sleep at night, those few minutes before you fall asleep, your filter faculty is completely shut down, at the same time your conscious mind is deeply relaxed and about to shut down, this means you are in that moment operating from the theta level. When you look at those images as your eyes are beginning to feel droopy and ready to close, those images become the last thing impressed onto the subconscious mind, this means that in that moment the subconscious mind sees those images as a reality.

The same thing happens when you first wake up and open your eyes, the conscious mind is just waking up and the filter faculty is still shut down, thus those images go straight onto your theta level of the subconscious. This reinforces the reality that the subconscious created the night before when you fell asleep. Magic will not happen immediately, this also needs time, give your subconscious mind at least two or three months to really create that new reality in a powerful way before you start to notice any real major changes.

To further enhance your success with the vision board, try and place pictures of the important goals you want to achieve first in a place of the vision board where it is the most dominant picture. You can place as many pictures on the vision board as you wish, it is the ones you focus on the most that will be achieved in shorter periods of time.

You can have both your short term and long term goals on your vision board, however your focus on them has to be equal. To further enhance your success with this, when you focus on a particular picture, try and put emotion into it, feeling the emotions and feelings of what it would feel like if you had it now.

For example, if you have a picture of your dream house on the vision board, state in your mind in an assertive manner, "I own this house" and get in touch with the feelings of what it would be like to own that dream house right now.

The purpose of this is to train your mind into believing it is possible to have that house right now. This increases belief in achieving that goal and motivating you toward achieving the goal. You can even create affirmations around those feelings of having that dream house now. Usually the best affirmations are the ones you create yourself, using power words that make it sound as if you already have it, especially words that resonate and feel good to you.

Keep the affirmation as short and simple as possible to make it easy to remember and say as many times as possible during the day. For example, "I own and live in my dream house" and while saying that, feel the emotions of what it would be like if you were in that house. The affirmation quoted here is stated in the positive and in the now, however those words specifically may not resonate with everyone on a subconscious level, therefore it is important that you create your own affirmations with words that make you feel good and resonate with you.

It can even be short as three or four words, "I own that house", simple and short. When you use short sentences like "I own that house" especially when you are away from your vision board during the day, make sure you have an image of the picture of the house on your mind while stating the affirmation, you can train yourself to have a mental image even with your eyes open.

Focus on the pictures on the vision board, combined with the emotions of having it now, with the affirmations will build a strong belief that it is possible to achieve the goal and eventually get you there. As this fantasy becomes a strong reality on the subconscious mind, the subconscious mind develops attitudes toward achieving that goal. Basically the subconscious mind must match what has become a reality on it to what exists in your life in the real world.

This does not mean that the dream house will magically appear in front of you, there are other steps you will have to take to achieve that. First you have to state and are clear of the area or suburb you want that dream house to be in. Get in touch with your feelings and really feel what it would be like living in that area or suburb.

You will notice opportunities that will start to creep up that will help you get the financial benefit of being able to buy or build that dream house. This is where the hard work comes in, those opportunities will come up many times, it is up to you to be alert to them and take action on it.

You will also notice that suddenly people will pop up into your life that are in positions to help you get closer to those opportunities or even offer you opportunities that will bring you the financial freedom you need to buy or build your dream house. It is your responsibility to check out those opportunities and to act on them.

Being responsible for your life and not attributing blame on anyone or anything is the most powerful tool you can create for yourself. Therefore if it feels as if the vision board is not working, first ask yourself "Am I fully focused on the picture every night and morning"? Remember you don't have to focus on a picture for longer than three minutes if you are in your theta state, the state you are usually in just before you fall asleep or when you first wake up.

The second question you need to ask yourself is "Am I really putting the correct emotion into this"?

The third question is "Do I have the correct words in my affirmation that resonate with me"? Trust your subconscious here. You will become intuitive to the answer to that question.

The fourth question you need to ask yourself is "Am I not alert to opportunities or am I letting them pass me by"? Sometimes the person you least expect, could be the person who would be able to direct you in the direction to achieving your goals.

The final question is "Am I taking the necessary actions"? There are no real failures in life other than the failure to take action. The vision board is a very good tool for non-visual people as well. Non-visual people can focus on the pictures on the board and allow themselves to feel the emotions of having it now.

Fall asleep with those emotions and affirmations in your thoughts. When you wake up, focus on the picture and call up the emotions again, try and keep those emotions going for as long as possible after you wake up. When you are using your affirmations during the day, try and call up the emotions of having it now while stating your affirmations.

Visualisation

Like vision boards, visualization works best when put directly onto the subconscious mind when in the theta level, this is the state that you are in just before you go to sleep or when you just wake up. Visualization on the theta level does have an added advantage over the vision board.

People who can visualize will find that they have an added advantage because they can go to the theta level at any time during the day with the right exercises. Visualization is usually done with the eyes closed and has the advantage of creating the images with motion and in real time, thus creating a stronger feeling of having it now which increases belief in achieving that goal.

There are two methods you can use to visualize, one is to visualize the goal as if you are watching a movie on a screen and the other is visualizing it as if you are in that movie. Both are powerful but the latter will help increase the feeling of having it now. Visualizing is not just seeing the images in 3D but also putting in the emotions of how you would feel if you had it now.

The feeling and vision has to be as strong and clear as possible for the subconscious mind to accept that new life and turn that fantasy into reality. Remember that this does not happen overnight; you have to keep visualizing that specific goal in the same way for as long as possible, preferably until the goal is achieved. The subconscious mind needs time to create the new attitude and belief that it is yours before it can start matching the fantasy into the real world.

It is important that you practice this every day for at least two or three months before you start to experience any real changes or movements toward that goal. However depending on how strong your vision is on the subconscious mind don't be surprised if things start to happen sooner. The goal is not just going to drop out of the sky like magic, you still have to be alert to opportunities and take action especially when you feel inspired to do so. Remember your mind will not fail you; the only failure is the failure to be in action.

The key to strong visualization is to plan it out like you would create a plot for a movie, difference being that your little movie should not be longer than ten minutes. Five to ten minutes is adequate for these movies of the mind because if it goes on longer than that, the mind could wander and lose focus.

When there is loss of focus the picture changes and that could cause confusion on your subconscious mind of what the actual end result of the desired goal really is. This will either lead to the goal not being realised or to achieving less than what is truly possible. In truth, what the mind conceives it will achieve.

Visualization is actual movies of the mind with you playing the lead role. These little movies require as much detail as possible and are created in positive context as if the goal has already been achieved, the end result of the desire or goal. The mind movie must contain all the emotions of what it would feel like to have the desire or goal now, sounds that you may think you will hear, the exact place where the goal will be achieved, whether you will be alone or there will be others, including touch, taste and smell, basically to increase that emotion of having it now, it's best to use all five senses.

The short movie of the mind should look as real as possible when being visualized on the theta level so as to create it in real time for stronger motivation and belief of being able to achieve that goal and even going beyond that. The more focus put into it the stronger your chances of achieving that goal.

This may seem like hard work, it probably would be for some especially when having to think out the plot of the little movie. However remember that this is your little movie and you can make it fun and enjoyable as only you are going to see it because it will only be run or viewed in your mind.

The first step is to list all your short and long term goals. The next step is to decide which are the most important goals and list them in order of importance. If you have quite a number of goals, choose the first three short term goals you want to achieve. Work on these three goals first so that you can train yourself to achieve goals faster than you used to do before. You can then choose one long term goal to work on simultaneously.

The visualization for the short term goals should be three to five minutes and the long term goal should be ten minutes to enable you to put in more detail. The three short term goals can be visualized first thing in the morning when you have just woken up. This is quite a powerful time for short term goals. The long term goal can be visualized at night as you fall asleep so as to fall asleep with that goal on your mind. These are the two best times to get straight into your theta level.

When you have just woken up, sit up in your bed, take in a deep breath, let it out slowly and close your eyes again. Avoid staying in the lying position; you want to avoid falling asleep again. Once the eyes are closed, visualize your first short term goal as if you have already achieved it, using all your senses in this movie of the mind.

Try to avoid dwelling too long on the first one, once you feel as if three or four minutes have gone by, allow the image to fade and let your mind go blank. When the mind feels or seems completely blank, start to visualize the second goal in the same way as the first.

Once you feel that three or four minutes have passed, allow that image to fade and let the mind go blank. Call up the third goal and visualize it. Once you feel three to four minutes have passed let it fade, go to a blank mind, take in a deep breath and let it out slowly through your mouth. Open your eyes and let all expectation related to those goals go.

Expectation brings disappointment, things will happen when you least expect them to. Try and keep those good and positive emotions you felt while visualizing your goals for as long as you can or throughout the day if possible. Believe that you deserve and will achieve those goals but don't put any expectations on them rather just let it happen. You can specify a date by when you would like to achieve specific goals but make those dates within realistic time frames for achievement.

This means to allow yourself three to six months to achieve those goals unless they are really small goals that can be achieved within days. Every time you start to feel a little down or negative emotion, you can either use one of the techniques on emotional detachment or call up all the positive emotions that you felt with visualizing your goals.

Once you achieve your first goal, remember that emotion and add it to all your other visualizations. Achieving your first goal will be the motivating factor in getting you into action to achieve your other goals faster. Have fun and allow yourself to enjoy the process, it will make things a lot easier.

The little movie of the mind that you create must be focused on the end result. This means that you have to visualize what you want as if you have already achieved it. There should be as much detail in it as possible; this is done using all five senses if necessary or possible.

At first it might seem or could even be a little difficult to use all five senses, this is normal. Start with seeing the end result or achieved goal. Thereafter put in emotion, how would you feel if you have it now? Once you are able to feel the emotion as strong as possible, you can then bring in the sense of touch.

As you are seeing your goal, if your goal is an object, what would it feel like in your hands? You don't have to use the sense of touch if the goal is a new job, however try and create the feeling of what it would feel like to run your hand over the desk at the new job, this is only an option to increase your sensory acuity towards achieving goals.

Once you have built up the sense of feeling the emotion and touch, bring in the sense of sound, does the object have a sound? What do you think you would hear others say once you have achieved the goal? Try to imagine hearing others complementing you on your achievement, even if it is a small goal. Try to identify if there will be any scents or smells associated with the goal and try and create the sense of smelling what it would be like if it was there right in front of you.

Normally you would not need the sense of taste especially if the goal is not food, however you can imagine what you would be celebrating the goals with in terms of what you would like to eat or drink once you have achieved that goal, this part is only optional but will help to increase sensations that will help you create the belief that anything is possible.

Work on bringing in one sense at a time if you have not done this before. Once you have achieved bringing in all your senses into your visualization, you can then create the final mind movie on how it would really be if you had that goal achieved now.

At this point, you probably will notice that your mind movie is more than ten minutes long, therefore refine that mind movie so that it is shorter than ten minutes and the main focus is on having achieved the goal. Initially this will seem like a lot of work, however using imagination and visualization can be a lot of fun especially if you put a lot of passion into it. Therefore it is important to identify how passionate are you toward achieving that goal?

There are a number of things that you have to take note of when creating your mind movies. There is no need to worry if you don't get it right the first time; you have creativity within you which will come up as you get into the process of visualising. Initially you may not know exactly what you want, that is okay, therefore give yourself some time to get to that final image.

In the first couple of weeks you may want to change things in the visualization or mind movie. There is no problem with that, once you have made the final decision of exactly what you want, stick to that final mind movie and visualize it at least once a day, preferably three times a day, until you have achieved the goal.

Remember the mind movie does not have to be too long, only five or ten minutes, therefore three times a day should not be too difficult to do. As you create these mind movies, you will notice just how creative you can really be. Allow your imagination to flow; this will aid you in developing some really good ideas.

The more imaginative and creative you are, the more creative you will be with ideas in the future especially after having achieved your first three goals. You must be relaxed when performing or creating the mind movies in order to get to that theta level, therefore the best time to start is just before you go to sleep or when you just wake up.

Note that if you have consumed alcohol even if it is just one or two glasses of wine, you will struggle to get into the theta state. It is recommended that when you do your visualization exercises, make sure you have not consumed alcohol for at least five to six hours. The reason for this is that alcohol is a stimulant that can put you into an alternate mind set and prohibit you from having full sensory acuity while developing these mind processes. You can drop it to four hours once you have achieved at least two goals because by then your mind will be trained in using those visualizations especially if they are used on a regular basis.

Another aspect to take note of, especially in the initial stages of creating visualizations, is that if you consume a lot of red meat, make sure that you wait at least two or three hours before trying to get into the theta level. Consumption of excess of red meats requires the digestive system to work a little harder than normal. This could cause the brain to move higher in the beta state and sometimes red meat does make the body temperature a little higher than normal during the digestive process.

This could make you feel uncomfortable and disturb you at the theta level, remember that the body and mind has to be completely relaxed when going into the theta level for visualizing your goal and making it powerful directly on the subconscious mind.

Two Examples

Here are two examples of a mind movie which are based on getting a new house and car. These examples are just guidelines; your mind movie will be unique to you. Therefore do not doubt yourself and just relax and be imaginative, you do have more creativity then you think you do.

You are standing in the street in front of your dream home based in the suburb or area of your dreams. You start to walk up the driveway and notice all the beautiful flowers and trees in the front garden. You begin to smell all the sweet scents of the flowers and notice all the different colours of flowers and where each flower bed is situated.

You notice the luscious green lawn and little garden ornaments around the area. Suddenly you can hear the birds chirping in the tree which sounds so melodious to you. You notice the colour of the walls of the front of the house, the number of windows on the front of the house and the porch leading up to the front door.

You notice the beautiful tiling on the front steps leading up to the front door and the colour and position of the front door. You walk up the steps and over the porch to the front door. You open the door and walk inside, taking note of the entrance hall, its colour scheme, floor tiles and the different entrances leading to the other rooms.

As you walk through the house, you see the exact curtains or blinds that you always wanted on the windows. You notice all the furniture that you want, its colours and exact positions. You see the kitchen that you always wanted in its exact colour scheme and layout. As you walk through each room you notice that every room has the furniture you always wanted in the exact position that you want it to be.

All the rooms are the exact colour scheme that you want. You can now smell some soft fragrances around the house in flower vases placed in just the right place. You take one more walk around the house enjoying each moment knowing that this is your house. You begin to feel the emotion of joy knowing that you finally have your dream home.

You walk out into the back yard and notice the back garden, its flowers and trees. Smelling the fresh fragrances of the flowers and hearing the melodious chirping of the birds. While you are feeling all those exciting emotions of having this dream house now, with a big smile on your face you silently say thank you two or three times.

At this point let the picture fade then fall asleep with all those good emotions. If you are visualising that when you have just woken up, take a deep breath and open your eyes slowly and try and keep those good emotions for as long as you can throughout the day.

Take note of the words that you use while creating this mind movie. Avoid using words like "I need", for example "I need a desk placed next to the window in the study", change that to "I want the desk placed next to the window in the study". State exactly what you want and where you want it. Avoid sentences like "I would like" or "I think it would be nice if", be clear on what you want and state it assertively. The language around your visualization is just as important and stating it assertively reinforces what you really want on your subconscious mind.

Visualising the new car requires that you know exactly what make and model of car you want. You have to know the exterior colour as well as the interior trim, whether it is leather or cloth, what accessories you want on the car. Therefore it is best you first do your research on the exact car you want and what colours and trims it comes in, what accessories are available with that particular car? Do not be afraid to dream big therefore the following example is based on a sports car. Remember this is just an example, you will know your car when you see it because it is unique to you just as unique as you are.

You come out of your house and there is a red Porsche 911 Turbo parked in your driveway. You can feel the key in your hand as the excitement builds up to drive the car for the first time. You admire its shape and take a good look at its mag wheels and then notice the glass sliding sunroof.

You open the driver's door and immediately get that new leather smell coming from the interior. You see the black leather interior and slide into the driver's seat. You notice the brushed aluminium inserts in the door panels and the dashboard. It has a navigation screen in the upper centre console where you can select your radio station or music that you want to hear. You start the car and hear the engine fire up just perfectly.

You put the car into reverse and slowly back out of the driveway. You drive down the street with a smile on your face enjoying the moment of having this new car. You are aware of all those good emotions as you drive to your favourite place. You can hear the sound of the engine as you drive enjoying every moment with feelings of gratitude of having achieved this goal. You drive back to your driveway, turn the car off, get out of the car with a huge smile and walk back into your home feeling empowered.

At this point let the picture fade slowly and go to sleep with those emotions while letting your mind clear. If you have just woken up and visualizing that, make sure you are sitting up and when the picture fades, take in a deep breath and as you let it out, open your eyes slowly and try and maintain those good emotions throughout the day.

It is important that you know exactly what you want so as to visualize it in the correct context. Be positive and believe that you are deserving of having it now especially while visualizing. The slightest doubt could be the obstacle from achieving that goal. Anything is possible if you believe it to be, however it is also about keeping the practice of the exercises and taking action when inspired to do so.

The purpose of holding the good emotions throughout the day will keep you in a positive state of mind which will draw you to opportunities that will help you achieve those goals. As you develop your skills you will begin to become alert to opportunities or even come up with great ideas that will create those opportunities.

Stay focused on the end result and never question how or when it will happen, this will cause doubt and block you from achieving those goals. Give yourself reasonable time to achieve those goals and always believe you are deserving of it.

Never be afraid to dream big because big dreams do come true provided you are willing to take the actions toward them. You can add to the belief of having those goals achieved by acting as if you already have it, this helps to further develop your sensory acuity towards creating greater ideas towards better opportunities. Most important, never doubt yourself as you are much more powerful than you think you are.

Chapter 10
Accessing Your Theta Level

Although the best times to access the theta level are just before you go to sleep or in the morning when you have just woken up, you can access the theta level at any time during the day with the right relaxation exercises. These relaxing techniques are fairly simple and take up to three minutes to perform.

You will know that you are in the theta level when you are completely relaxed and feel a little sleepy. Therefore if you are going to access the theta level during the day between the times you wake up and go to sleep, it is best done in the sitting position to avoid falling asleep.

If you choose to take a power nap during the day, you can access the theta level as you fall into the nap and visualize your goal for the first three minutes falling asleep with that vision on your mind. This really helps with training your mind to have what it is that you really want, developing attitudes and behaviours to achieve those goals.

The technique is fairly simple but it is up to you to create the discipline to keep practicing it for the purposes of achieving your goals. Initially it might seem like extra work especially if you have not done it before, this might cause you to have some resistance toward practicing the exercise.

If you do find yourself resisting the practice of getting to the theta level, ask yourself, "How passionate am I toward achieving this goal and how much do I want it?" There has to be a desire, a plan and the willingness to do the work if you really want something badly enough. The question is not whether it will work but are you willing to do the work?

Accessing Theta

To access your theta level, find a quiet place where you can sit comfortably and not be disturbed. Sit straight up in the chair; make sure your spine is straight, with your feet flat on the floor. Place your palms on your lap making sure that your arms and legs are not crossed.

Take a deep breath through your nose and hold it for three seconds then gently let it out of your mouth. Take a second deep breath, a little deeper than the first one, hold it for three seconds and then gently let it out of your mouth.

Now take in a third deep breath, as deep as possible, hold it and as you hold your breath, let your eyes close gently, then let the breath out of your mouth as slowly and gently as possible.

Now start to breathe deeply and gently in and out of your nose. Concentrate on your deep breathing for at least thirty seconds. At this point you should be feeling as if your body is starting to relax. After focusing on your deep breathing for thirty seconds, by this time your mind should be blank and the only thing is the focus on the breathing. If it feels as if your mind is not blank or your body is not completely relaxed, go back to focusing on your deep breathing in and out of your nose.

Once you feel relaxed and your mind feels blank, draw your attention to the top of your head keeping your eyes closed. Only draw your attention to the top of your head, do not visualize it. Once your attention is at the top of your head, say in your mind "All the tiny muscles in my scalp and back of my head are completely and deeply relaxed." Try to avoid thinking if the muscles are really relaxed or not, just trust the process, your body will respond to your suggestions.

Now draw your attention to your forehead stating "All the muscles in my forehead are relaxed". Now draw your attention to your temples and cheeks stating "all the muscles in my face are relaxed". Now draw your attention to your eyes stating "All the tiny muscles in my eyes are relaxed". "The tiny muscles in my eyes are so relaxed that my eyes just want to stay shut".

Now draw your attention to your jaw and state "all my jaw muscles are completely relaxed". Next draw your attention to your neck stating "All the muscles in my neck and shoulders are completely relaxed". Now draw your attention to your upper arms and state "All the muscles in my upper arms going into my elbows and forearms are completely relaxed".

Draw your attention to your wrists and hands and state "All the muscles in my wrist going into my hands, palms and right into my finger tips are completely relaxed." Now draw your attention to your chest area and state "All the muscles in my chest and upper back are completely relaxed".

Draw your attention to the abdominal area stating "All the muscles in my abdominal area and lower back are completely relaxed". Draw your attention to your hips stating "All the muscles in my hips, going into my thighs and behind my knees are completely relaxed".

Draw your attention to your calves stating "All my muscles in my calves, going into my ankles, my upper feet and right into the tip of my toes are completely relaxed". Draw your attention to the souls of your feet stating "The souls of my feet and every muscle in my body are completely relaxed".

Now go back to focusing on your deep breathing in and out of your nose allowing your mind to go blank. At this point you should be feeling completely relaxed. Trust the process and don't delve on whether your muscles are relaxed or not, that whole exercise should not take you more than a minute or two. The good news is that if you practice this exercise every day, after three months every time you sit in a comfortable position and breathe deeply, you just have to say the word relax and your muscles will automatically respond.

You are breathing deeply in and out of your nose, your body is now completely relaxed and your mind is blank. Allow your imagination to flow now and imagine that you are starting to float upwards slowly and gently, feeling comfortable and safe.

Imagine that you are floating upwards into the sky higher and higher past the atmosphere. Imagine you are floating into space, into the quiet depths of the universe. You are completely relaxed and engulfed by the vastness and emptiness of the universe, there is nothing to see everything is just blank. Now slowly allow the image of your goal to come up and begin to visualize the mind movie that you have created.

If floating into the universe does not work for you, try imagining that you are walking down stairs. Create the stairs as big and even as beautiful as you want it to be, it can be indoors or outdoors. Imagine that there are twenty five stairs going down and as you start to walk down the stairs, say the word deeper in your mind and repeat that word deeper every four or five steps down.

When you get to the bottom of the staircase imagine that you have entered a beautiful and brightly lit hall. There is no furniture just an empty hall with beautiful paintings on the wall. Imagine walking to the other side of the hall toward a door at the opposite end of the staircase you have just come down. Imagine walking through the door into a warm room, just at the right temperature.

The room has a large window with a beautiful view. You can create that view to be a beautiful garden, landscape or beach, whatever makes you feel good. Imagine there is a very comfortable recliner facing the window and you walk over and sit in it.

As you look out into the beautiful view that you have created, let the image change from that view to the goal you want to achieve. Visualize your goal for five or ten minutes. Once you have gone through the mind movie you have created, using all your senses, allow the picture to fade and go back to focusing on breathing deeply in and out of your nose until your mind feels blank again.

Then take in a deep breath and hold it for three seconds and let it out slowly through your mouth. Take in a second deep breath through your nose and as you hold it, slowly open your eyes and blink a few times then let the breath slowly out of your mouth. Take in a final deep breath but don't hold it this time just slowly let it out of your mouth. Stand up and give yourself a good stretch.

Initially this whole process may take up to fifteen minutes especially if you are doing it for the first time. However be patient with yourself, let your mind get used to it, within a few days you will notice that you are able to do it in less than ten minutes.

If you are someone who meditates regularly, you probably can leave out the relaxing technique of going through each muscle to relax them because your body automatically relaxes when in meditation. Meditation is probably one of the best and powerful ways to get into theta. You may use meditation for spiritual or mindfulness purposes, however I have found that it can be quite powerful to add five or ten minutes to your meditation to visualize your goal towards the end of each meditation because meditation gets you into theta state..

The advantage that meditation has is that it helps you have a more alert mind and recognising opportunities or coming up with great ideas is much easier. I use meditation for visualising my goals and have found it creates a stronger belief in achieving the goal as well as a stronger motivation to work toward taking action when inspired to do so.

The other advantage that meditation offers is that it develops a calmness in you that lasts throughout the day. When you are constantly calm, there is no stress, it becomes easier to identify possible solutions to obstacles, solving problems becomes much easier and quicker to resolve. Meditation is not just about spirituality or religion but about becoming mindful in creating a better life in a holistic way. It might sound esoteric to some but the reality is that the real meaning of meditation is being in a relaxed state with a clear mind. It is what you use or do in the meditation that becomes esoteric, spiritual or religious and so on. Meditation can be a very powerful tool to achieving goals as well.

For those who struggle to visualize; you learnt previously that you can use your imagination to work with your other senses to get a sense of what you want to achieve, like feeling it rather than seeing it. This may not be as strong as vivid visualization but it does help to create the feeling of having it now which increases belief and motivation in achieving that goal.

There are exercises that you can use to train yourself to visualize. Training your mind to visualize is not a quick fix exercise and will take some discipline and dedication. Being able to visualize vividly is a great tool to have and sometimes going through the process of training your mind to visualize can be rewarding. The process can take quite a number of months therefore realistically allow for six months to train your mind to visualize.

This does not mean in any way that you have to put your goals on hold until you have trained your mind to visualize. There are other options you can use to achieve your goals simultaneously while training your mind to visualize. Be patient and you will definitely notice the benefits in the long run.

Train your Mind to Visualize

There are two options you can use to train your mind to visualize. You can choose the option that best suits you or you can use both on alternate days.

The first option is a fairly simple exercise but requires a good length of time for it to really be effective. It is quite an effective option provided you are willing to put in the effort to practice for at least fifteen minutes a day for as long as possible.

The first step is to choose a picture that you like the most, a picture of an object if the goal is an object you want to get. Alternatively you can use a photo of someone you love. Place the picture in front of you at eye level or slightly higher. Keep your head straight with the eyes focused forward at the picture. If the picture is slightly higher than eye level, do not lift your chin up, move only your eyes up so as to get focused on the picture.

The purpose of having the picture slightly higher than eye level helps to increase memory and developing a stronger possibility of being able to visualize vividly. If at first you find you are feeling strained by having the picture slightly higher than eye level, bring it back down to eye level and start with that and then build it up to having it slightly higher than eye level with only the eyes focused upward.

Once you find yourself in a comfortable position being able to focus directly on the picture, stare at the picture for ten minutes and try not to lose focus on staring at the picture throughout the ten minutes. You might want to get a timer for this exercise. After ten minutes of staring at the picture, immediately close your eyes and notice if you are able to see that exact image on your mind or mind's eye.

It does not have to be one hundred percent clear. This is the first time you are doing this. If there is no image when your eyes are closed, do not let that discourage you, open your eyes and try again the next day. If there is an image, try and hold that image on your mind's eye for at least five minutes. Keep practicing this exercise for as many days as possible until you are able to get a clear image and keep it on your mind for a full five minutes.

Once you are able to hold the image for at least five minutes on your mind, choose another picture and repeat the process, you will notice this time that the process of seeing the image of the new picture will go much quicker.

Once you are able to see the image of the second picture on your mind for five minutes, try and see if you can bring up both images on your mind at the same time. Once you are able to visualize both pictures on your mind at the same time, the next step is to imagine the pictures moving to different spots in the mind eye. When you have achieved that, imagine the pictures are in motion moving around your mind while you are able to see them clearly.

This last part may take some time to work but just keep at it you will enjoy the benefits later. Once you are able to see the pictures in motion, try and create a 3D image of each picture and work on that in the same way until you can see them in motion.

Once you are able to see the 3D images in motion you can then add sound and feeling to them until they start to feel very real or vivid to you. The final step is to bring in more pictures and work with them until you are able to see them in 3D. Once you have done the process two or three times, you will notice that with practice it will get much easier and quicker to do.

Once you are able to see many pictures at the same time in 3D and in motion, you are now ready to create that mind movie. Avoid letting this feel like a chore, have fun with it. If it does not work for you, it does not mean that there is something wrong with you. Some will get it right and others won't, that is just the way it is.

However do not despair if it does not work for you, there are other options that will be of great advantage to you.

Another Option

The second option to train your mind to visualize requires more use of your imagination. The advantage of this option is that you can really get in tune with your creativity. This is not going to be a short term process and will require time, dedication and perseverance. Initially you can start with fifteen minutes a day, thereafter building it up to at least thirty minutes or more a day.

This option will seem like hard work and probably will even feel like that especially in the beginning, some people will try and avoid using this option and others may even give up within a week or two. The question is; are you willing to improve on your ability to visualize or be imaginative and creative? How passionate are you toward your goal and wanting to achieve it? Are you willing to do what it takes to build on your imagination and creativity?

There is no short cut with this one and may not seem like fun to do but it will really get you in tune with your ability to be creative and come up with some great ideas. This option will also help you develop sensory acuity which will benefit you in many ways, especially with helping you identify possible solutions to problems.

The first step is to train yourself to be completely still for at least fifteen minutes. You may want to use a timer with this exercise. First find a comfortable chair that will support your back as you want to be sitting straight up with the spine straight. Make sure that you will not be disturbed during this time and you are able to get at least fifteen minutes of quiet time.

Initially you might want to place an object in front of you to focus on while training yourself to be absolutely still. The aim of this exercise is to train your body and mind to be completely quiet and relaxed so as to access the most creative part of you. Once you have your comfortable chair in a quiet place, this place can be indoors or outdoors, whatever is comfortable for you and makes you feel happy and calm.

Sit in your chair with the back up straight and your feet flat on the floor. Put your palms on your lap either facing down or up, whatever is comfortable for you. Take in a deep breath through your nose and let it out of your mouth slowly and then repeat it another two times. You don't have to close your eyes for this part of the exercise.

Once you feel completely comfortable, try to stay absolutely still in that position for at least fifteen minutes. You can focus on an object if you want to and it does not matter whether your mind wonders or not, the aim is only to train yourself to be absolutely still at this point. If you find that you are unable to be still for fifteen minutes, don't beat yourself up about it, it is okay. Time yourself on how long you are able to be still then build it up from there by adding a minute each day until you get to fifteen minutes.

For example if you find that you are only able to be absolutely still for nine minutes, end the session and wait until the next day. The next day set the timer for ten minutes and practice ten minutes each day until you are still for the whole ten minutes. After that from the following day set the timer for eleven minutes and try and be absolutely still for the whole eleven minutes.

Then build on there by adding a minute each time you reach your target. If you are able to take out thirty minutes of your day to practice this, ideally it would benefit you greatly if you can train yourself to be absolutely still for thirty minutes or more.

Once you are able to be absolutely still for at least fifteen minutes, the next step is to train your mind to stop wandering. First start with focusing on an object and stay focused on that object without thinking about anything for at least fifteen minutes. Time yourself first to see how long you can keep focused on the single object.

If you are unable to stay focused on the object for fifteen minutes don't beat yourself up about it. Stop the session and then try again the next day. You can repeat the exercise by building it up by one minute each day like when you trained yourself to be still. For example if you are only able to stay focused on the object for six minutes, end the session then the next day try to stay focused for seven minutes. Build it up by a minute each time you reach your target until you get to fifteen minutes.

If you are able to spend more time with this try to build it up to thirty minutes or even an hour, this will be of great benefit to you especially in the area of creativity and problem solving. Once you are able to keep your body still and mind focused on the one object without thinking of anything or letting your mind wander for fifteen minutes, the next step is to try and be still with a clear mind without focusing on the object and with the eyes closed.

Once you start with being still with the eyes closed, it is natural for your mind to wander because it had become accustomed to focusing on an object with the eyes open. However it should not take you long to train your mind to be still with the eyes closed because you have already created that ability to be still.

Once you have got to the point where you are able to be still physically and mentally for at least fifteen minutes, try to build it up to twenty then thirty minutes. Getting to this point may take at least a month or two; however this is also an opportunity for you to train yourself to have patients and discipline.

This may seem like a long time to you but the end result will be of great benefit especially when it comes to working on big and long term goals. Although this exercise is to help non visual people to develop the ability to visualize or have strong sensory acuity, it will help visual people who practice this to develop their ability to get into theta faster and stay there longer, as well as helping them develop sharper and more detailed images that would be of great benefit to them.

For those of you who are non-visual, it does not mean that you cannot get started or move on with your goals while you are working on developing visual or sensory acuity skills. You have the vision board to work with and there will be other options that you will learn in further chapters.

A good way to train your mind to be still with your eyes closed is on the first day while you sit absolutely still for thirty minutes, just let your mind wander without trying to stop it. The next day, try and keep all your thoughts clear for at least three minutes and then just let your mind wonder for the next twenty seven minutes.

From there try and build it up by two minutes each day until you get to thirty minutes. If you find that after eight weeks of practicing this exercise that you are able to be still for at least thirty minutes but are still struggling to keep your mind quiet for more than fifteen minutes, don't beat yourself up about it, just move on to the next step.

Once you have developed the ability to be still and clear your mind for thirty minutes or more, the next step is to find a comfortable place to sit where you have a blank wall in front of you. If you have been doing this exercise outdoors up until now, it would be better to now move indoors and find a place where you can sit in front of a blank wall.

Once you have found a comfortable place in front of a blank wall, estimate where the centre of the wall is, you don't have to be accurate, only an estimate of the centre is required. Now focus on this perceived centre with your eyes straight ahead and try and stay still for thirty minutes while focusing on this perceived centre of the wall.

The next day do the same. Focus on this perceived centre of the wall but this time without moving your eyes from that perceived centre try and get the whole area of that wall into your visual perimeters. Use a timer for this one, after fifteen minutes imagine that there is a tiny black dot on that centre where your eyes are focused. At the end of that second fifteen minute session, blink your eyes a few times and wait until the next day.

On the third day, imagine that perceived centre once again with that tiny dot you imagined the day before. The perceived centre does not have to be the same spot each day so don't worry about remembering where you have located the perceived centre as long as you feel you are focusing on the centre of the wall.

Once you are focused on this tiny dot in the centre of the wall, using a timer every five minutes, imagine that the tiny dot gets a little bigger. Repeat this until you have completed your thirty minute session. The next day imagine that tiny dot on the centre of the wall and then every three minutes imagine it gets bigger until you have completed your thirty minute session.

The following day do the same with the dot getting bigger every minute until your thirty minutes are complete, it does not matter if that tiny dot grows to the point where it covers the whole wall, the idea here is to train your mind to visualize. The following day, imagine that the tiny dot on the centre of the wall gets bigger every few seconds until it is big enough to cover most of the wall.

Once you have achieved that then imagine that the dot is now getting smaller every few seconds until it is a tiny dot on the centre of the wall again. Practice for another two days making that tiny dot become as big as the wall every few seconds and then back down to being a dot again as many times as possible in that thirty minute session.

Once you are successful with making the circle bigger and smaller on the wall, the next step is to imagine that small dot on the centre of the wall again. This time imagine that the small dot is extending out of the wall like a needle or stick extending out of the wall towards you. You don't have to extend it out too far, about half a meter is good, also don't worry about being accurate on the measurements.

Imagine the dot extending out toward you and then back into the wall until you only see the dot. Do this at least ten times then when you see it as just a dot on the wall again, imagine it becoming bigger like a circle on the wall, it does not have to be too big.

Now imagine that the circle is extending out of the wall and forming a cone shape on the wall. Imagine it going back into the wall and being a circle again. Do this a few times until you feel you are able to imagine the circle extending out into a cone and back in again quickly and clearly.

Once you are able to do this, take a break and come back the next day for the next step. The next step is to imagine the dot on the centre of the wall growing into a circle then extending out of the wall in a cone shape then back into a circle on the wall. Remember you have been imagining this as a black dot that becomes a black circle.

Now when it is a circle on the wall again, change the colour of the circle to orange and then yellow. Try and imagine the circle changing colours for at least ten minutes. Now imagine the circle extending out of the wall into a cone shape, now imagine the cone changing colours. Once you have achieved that, you are ready for the next step.

The next step is to imagine a picture on the wall, a picture of a building or scenery would be best. You are still training yourself to be visual at this point so don't worry if you do not get a clear picture in your mind. Now in your mind create a short story or fairy tale around that picture you imagine on the wall, the story does not have to be visual, you just have to narrate it to yourself for a few minutes.

Now close your eyes and try to see if you can see the imagined picture on the wall in your mind's eye. Practice this step until you feel you have a clear enough picture. You might not be able to see the picture in your mind at this point but notice how strong the sense of the picture is on your mind. Keep practicing this step until you have a clear picture or very strong sense of it.

Once you have achieved that, close your eyes and try to imagine that you are standing in front of a high building. You are about a hundred feet away from the building. Take note of the exterior of the building. Now imagine that the exterior walls have disappeared and the building is getting smaller one floor at a time until there is nothing there but an empty plot. Now imagine the building coming up again until it is that whole building in front of you once more. Once you are able to do this, take a break from the session and start again the next day.

Once you have achieved that, compliment yourself and give yourself a big smile as well, this will be good for your subconscious mind. Now imagine a big piece of land with a house in the centre of it. Imagine that you are floating over this land into the house. Imagine the room you are in and placing furniture that you really like. Now imagine that there is someone in the room with you, anyone you like. Imagine you are having a conversation with this person, hearing their response to your questions or comments. Try to hear them, their voice and what you would imagine they would say.

Once you have achieved that, imagine you are walking out into the garden and are able to smell the scent of the flowers. Once you have achieved that, imagine that you are smelling coffee and then end the session. Once you have achieved that, from this point on practice for a few days creating little stories with images on your mind.

Allow yourself some time to let the stories and pictures become clear on your mind. This may take a few days but it will get stronger with practice. When you have come to the point where you can create stories and visions of those stories on your mind, you are now ready to visualize your goals with accurate imagery.

Training your mind to visualize is not easy and does take a lot of time, despite all this time and effort there will be some people who won't be able to visualize vividly or even visualize at all. This does not mean they are not good enough or incapable of achieving anything.

The important fact is that they would have increased their sensory acuity and built on their imagination very powerfully. The increase of their ability to sense as opposed to seeing imagery will increase their intuitive ability to recognize opportunities and act upon it with prompt action.

Those who have practiced the exercises to train the mind to visualize, both visual and non-visual people, will notice an increase in their ability of being creative. Remember that visualization is only a tool in helping you be motivated in achieving your goal; it is the willingness on your part to practice the visualization exercise and the willingness to be in action toward your goals. At the end of the day it is all about how focused you are and how much passion and effort you are willing to put into your goals and dreams.

The reality is that you might not attain exactly what you visualize but something very close to it unless it is something like a house, car or objects that you are working towards. If the outcome is not exactly the way you visualized it, does not mean you have failed. The reality is that you have moved forward and achieved something.

The trick is not to measure how much further you have to go to achieve your goal but to look back and see how far and how much you have achieved until this point in getting toward your goal. Always acknowledge yourself for the achievements towards your goal no matter how small those achievements are. This acknowledgement is training your mind to have it now and at the same time creating the motivation to keep going toward achieving that goal.

Always visualize the end result of what it is you want to achieve and never ask how and when the goal will be achieved. Focus on the end result and start with what you have now to be able to take action to make that goal or dream a reality. There is nothing wrong with dreaming big even if you never get there, the real success is in how much you have already achieved even if it is only half of what that original big dream was. Celebrate your achievements and be passionate about what you want, your passion will be the motivation to attract success because success always follows your passion.

Chapter 11
Handwriting: A
Subconscious Language

Think back to the time when you were in primary school or earlier, the time when you first began to write. Remember how you had to learn how to write each letter first in upper case or caps and then in lower case? After you were able to write each letter of the alphabet you had learned how to write words and then sentences.

During this time you also learned different forms of handwriting until you developed your own unique form of handwriting. As you evolved during this time so did your handwriting evolve with you, until it became your current form of writing. Within a short period of time your unique handwriting became embedded in your subconscious mind and second nature to you when you were required to write something.

Today you don't have to think about how to formulate letters or connect them in sentences, you just take out a pen and write things down without having to think how to write, the letters just flow naturally into your unique handwriting every time. The same with signing your signature, it comes out the same way every time and is as unique to you as your finger prints.

You never have to think about it, you just write with perfect flow. The reason for this is that you are writing directly from your subconscious level. This ability to write directly from the subconscious level is a tool that non-visual people can really take advantage of. This does not mean that visual people cannot use it to make it work for them.

Writing can be therapeutic and help you to really get creative in identifying what it is that you really want to achieve. If you are one of those people who have found themselves typing on a computer keyboard ninety nine percent of the time as opposed to using your own handwriting, the typing has now become your subconscious handwriting and therefore you can use the keyboard as your tool for writing from the subconscious level. Note if you type fifty percent of the time and write the other fifty percent, it is best to use your handwriting for your goals.

You probably have heard or have been told thousands of times, write down your goals. Every teacher, coach or motivational speaker says the same thing "Write down your goals". There is a very good reason for this; writing down your goals in your own handwriting is the most powerful way to create the motivation you need to achieve that goal from a subconscious level.

When you write your goals in your own handwriting, your subconscious mind will accept that new concept or change with less resistance. When you think of your goals and ideas, you are usually thinking on the conscious or beta level, this usually faces resistance from the subconscious mind because of its previous programing.

However the moment you put pen to paper and start writing those ideas and goals down, you go straight to your subconscious level thus less resistance, this means that when you are writing those goals and ideas it is like putting suggestions straight onto your subconscious mind and the subconscious mind readily accepts that new concept or idea.

This all occurs at the alpha level and thus increasing the motivation toward achieving those goals. Another advantage that we have as human beings is that if we are able to go into the alpha or theta state and write our goals from that state, it becomes an even more powerful tool than vivid visualization and the vision board put together.

The best way to write down your goals in the theta level is to write those goals down at night just before you go to sleep when you are in the natural state of theta. The best time to write daily or short term goals is in the morning when you have just woken up. This is the most powerful option available to those people who are non-visual.

As powerful as writing down your goals may be, it is still good to have the vision board and to be able to visualize your goals at the theta level. This is so you can develop sensory acuity or the feeling of having it now for stronger motivation and achievement. Acting as if you already have it over and above visualizing and writing your goals down helps you overcome procrastination in taking action.

Remember there is no such thing as failure other than the failure to take action. You can also increase your creativity and imagination which in turn will increase your sensory acuity through writing. This to some extent will help you get relaxed and into your alpha state.

Through your handwriting you can also identify whether you are optimistic or pessimistic toward the goals that you want to achieve. Knowing this will help you re-look at that specific goal to see and identify how passionately you want to achieve that goal or if it is really something that you really want or not.

Your handwriting can be such an amazing way of getting feedback on how strongly you want to achieve your dreams and desires from a deep subconscious level, it communicates this back to you on different levels and therefore it is a powerful language of the subconscious mind.

Writing down your goals at the theta level, at the time when you are about to go to sleep, leaves an impression of those ideas or goals on your mind for longer periods of time helping you identify or be alert to opportunities that will lead you to achieving those goals.

Writing down your short term and daily goals in the morning when you have just woken up will give you the motivation you need to complete you're to do list for the day or be in action with regards to your short term goals. Non-visual people especially those who cannot get vivid images or have a strong sense of their goal on their mind, can further enhance their ability by reading their goals quietly to themselves at least three times a day.

This compensates for the inability to visualize. The correct manner to do this especially for long term goals is to read the long term goal quietly in the morning when you have just woken up. You can then read that goal quietly to yourself in the middle of the day and finally in the early evening. About thirty minutes before you go to sleep, end your day by reading out your goal aloud, not too loud that everyone hears you but just loud enough for you.

This may seem more work than visualizing, in reality it is about the same but puts you on the same advantage level as people who can visualize. Visual people can use this technique as well especially if they find that they are lacking in motivation to be in action.

The first step is to know exactly what you want, most people know what they don't want and when you ask them, "What is it that you really want?" They usually sit looking at you with blank faces. During this process of identifying what you really want, with certain goals or things you will discover that some of the goals or things you thought you wanted were not really what you wanted but things that someone else convinced you was too good to have or achieve.

Some people even base their goals on following the trends of others or what they see around them rather than going for something they really like, or because they are afraid of what others may think. Therefore when writing down your goals, be as clear as possible with yourself that the object or goal that you want to get or achieve is actually something that you really want.

Once you are clear on what it is you really want, you will face less resistance from your subconscious mind and you will find that you become inspired in taking passionate action toward achieving that goal.

You can identify how you feel or what your mood is in the moment towards something through your handwriting. When you write down your thoughts and ideas consciously, you will get an ideomotor response from your sub-conscious mind reflected in your handwriting, symbolising how you really feel about those thoughts or how much you believe it to be true or not.

Your subconscious mind will reflect in your handwriting whether you are pessimistic or optimistic towards your goals. However your mood in the moment of writing can also reflect negative or positive traits and that may not be a true reflection of what you really feel or want with regards to achieving your goals. For example if you are in a negative or angry mood in the moment, your handwriting will reflect negativity towards that goal. Therefore it is important that before writing any goals down, you take the time to clear your mind of any thoughts that may be affecting you that could have arisen from situations that may have occurred during the day.

It is also good to check your emotions on how you are feeling in the moment, noticing whether you are feeling positive or negative, which could have probably been caused during the day due to specific situations or events. When you are writing down your goals, it is so important that you are clear on what it is that you want and that there are no other thoughts or feelings other than those thoughts and feelings directed towards your goals in that moment of writing.

Remember that your subconscious is a very powerful part of you and influences the outcomes of what you want or are thinking. Therefore if you are writing your goals and dreams while in a negative state caused by something or an event that may not even be related to your goals and dreams, the subconscious mind will trigger a negative reaction or outcome towards those goals and dreams no matter how positive you may be toward them.

Therefore it is a good idea to test how you feel towards your goals by writing them down while fully awake during the day and noticing whether you are optimistic or pessimistic towards those goals. This is done before you write down your actual goals in the alpha or theta state.

To identify whether you are optimistic or pessimistic towards your goal is fairly simple but bear in mind that when you are writing, the handwriting could also be reflecting your mood or emotions in that moment and therefore you may not be able to accurately know exactly how optimistic or pessimistic you really are toward that goal. The aim here is to only have a basic idea of how you feel about specific goals and whether it really is what you want or not.

If you do want an accurate reading with regards to how you perceive that goal, you can refer your handwriting samples to a trained handwriting analyst or graphologist. However going the professional route to identify how optimistic or pessimistic you are towards your goals is not necessary unless you are really in a space where you really have no idea of what it is you really want or would like to achieve in life.

Writing your goals and dreams

Once you have a clear idea of what it is that you really want, take some time out and find a quiet place where you can sit and write out your goals and dreams. Get a blank piece of paper that has no lines. Sometimes it is good to use your favourite type of stationery provided that the paper has no lines on it.

Once you are comfortable start writing down whatever comes to your mind, it does not matter what it is, positive or negative, something petty or something you may have been pondering about for a while, whatever it may be just write down your thoughts, this is to get rid of any negative emotions or thoughts that you may be feeling in the moment.

While you are writing all of this down, you will notice a change in your mood, it will start to get better because as you write, you start to get in touch with your creativity. It is really good from time to time to just sit and write your thoughts or anything that comes to mind in the moment, especially for non-visual people, this helps you to get deep into your imagination and creativity.

Once you have written down all those thoughts and ideas, take the sheet of paper and shred or burn it. This is a form of subconscious release of any negative emotions you may have been holding on to when starting to write that page. At this point you should be feeling some sense of relief and you are now ready to write down your goals and dreams to identify whether you are optimistic or pessimistic towards them. If you find that there is no change in your mood or that you feel nothing, that is perfectly okay and there is no need to worry about it, just move on to the next step anyway.

How do you feel about Your Goals?

Once you have shredded or burnt the sheet of paper with your thoughts, take another sheet of paper with no lines. Now write down your goals or dreams and try and write as many as possible so as to fill the sheet of paper.

At this time it does not matter whether you write the goals and dreams in present or future tense, the aim is merely to identify how you feel towards those goals and dreams. Try to keep the sentences short or in one line, but if they do go to the next line it is still okay.

Write down your most important goals and dreams, the ones that you feel strongly about achieving. You don't have to write every goal or dream, just enough to fill one sheet of paper. Once you have completed writing your goals and dreams, place the sheet of paper where the whole sheet is in line with your vision.

You will now look at the sentences as a line across the paper and not worry on how the sentences were constructed or if they are correct or not. Place a ruler under the first line or sentence, making sure that the ruler is absolutely straight or exactly parallel to the top edge of the sheet of paper. Once the ruler is placed correctly, notice if the first line that you wrote is straight, meaning it goes straight across the sheet. If so it indicates that you are balanced with your thoughts and emotions regarding your goals and dreams.

If the line you have written moves up slightly, meaning it starts straight but from the second word or from the middle of the line you wrote, moves up in a slight angle, it indicates that you are optimistic with regards to that goal and are willing to take action on it.

However if the line moves up at an angle where there is a large space from the edge of the ruler and the end of the line that you wrote, it indicates that you are either over optimistic with regards to your goal or dream or that your goal or dream is unrealistic.

It also could indicate that you subconsciously believe that your goal or dream is unobtainable. Check the angle of each line that you have written in the same way. Note the goals which you are balanced or optimistic with and the ones that you are over optimistic or unrealistic with.

Re-evaluate those goals, sometimes it may just mean that although you are optimistic towards that goal, you unconsciously believe that you cannot attain it. If this occurs, merely use a vision board to help you create a more realistic belief toward that goal or dream.

Re-evaluate those goals and dreams by really questioning whether it is what you really want and how much do you believe that you deserve it? Remember this is only an indication of how you subconsciously feel towards your goals and dreams. Do not get too hung up or depressed if you find that you are over optimistic or that your goal is unrealistic.

All you need to do is re-evaluate your thoughts and emotions around those goals and whether it is something you are truly passionate about. Tear up that sheet of paper and go and do something that makes you happy, otherwise use the first technique from chapter eight where you replace any negative emotions with positive ones.

Remember negative and positive emotions cannot be in the same place at the same time. Come back and re-write those goals and dreams and notice the difference, you will find that you either optimistic or more balanced in your thoughts and emotions towards those goals and dreams.

If you find that the lines you have written move downwards, meaning that the line starts straight but from the second word or the middle of the line it moves downwards so that the end of the sentence is lower than the start of the sentence, where the line is under the ruler, that is an indication that you are pessimistic toward that goal or dream.

The deeper the angle of the line you wrote the more pessimistic you are toward that goal. This would be a good time to evaluate your thoughts and emotions with regards to those specific goals and dreams. There could be a number of factors making you feel pessimistic towards those goals and dreams. Simply do the exercises from chapter eight on emotional detachment.

Sometimes there could have been a failure from the past that is making you feel pessimistic towards achieving new goals and dreams. Detach yourself emotionally from those past failures and let it go by writing them down and burning the sheet of paper.

Come back and re-write your goals and dreams. If you find at this point that you are still pessimistic towards your dreams and goals, this could indicate that you do not believe in yourself strong enough, feel you do not deserve this, you feel you are not good enough to achieve this goal or are merely just stuck in negative thoughts and emotions.

Another indication may be that you either have a fear of failure or a fear of success. Should this be the case re-evaluate your thoughts, words and emotions around those goals and dreams, are they positive enough?

Alternatively the best option would be to get a coach that can help you accurately identify whether you have the fear of success or failure, maybe even other fears that could be obstacles blocking you from wanting to achieve those goals and dreams.

Remember that this is just an indication and may not be one hundred percent accurate. You can train yourself to start believing in what you want by putting positive emotions into your dreams and goals, while using a vision board at the same time.

The more you write down those goals, you will notice that the pessimism will begin to move toward optimism. Avoid being hard on yourself and merely just keep working on being positive toward that which you want. A coach would be a healthy way to guide you to your path of success should you find that you are still struggling with being optimistic towards your goals and dreams.

There are other indicators or tell-tale signs, as I like to call it, that can help you identify how motivated you are towards taking action with regards to your goals and dreams. Take a look at the lines you have written across the page and notice if they form somewhat of a convex shape. This is where your first word starts to move up and then the line straightens, as you get to the end of the line the last two words seems to be in an angle moving downwards.

These convex lines indicate that you start with your goals with optimism and tend to slow down once you have gotten started and eventually there is no follow through, you never complete that goal. If the lines are concave shaped, meaning that the first word starts with a downward angle and then straitens towards the middle of the line, thereafter the line ends with the words towards an upward angle.

These concave lines indicate that you are pessimistic towards your goals at first, you procrastinate on getting started. It takes a while for you to get moving but once you do, you have strong momentum in completing that goal. If the lines are fairly straight it indicates that you are quite balanced in getting started and following through with your actions.

Overcoming Procrastination

If you are one of those who have momentum in getting started but end up procrastinating and having no follow through on achieving your goals, on the other hand if you are one of those who procrastinate on getting started and after a long while find momentum to get started and follow through, in both cases there is procrastination.

It is advisable that you consider working with a coach to help train you to be motivated in overcoming procrastination. It is not easy to overcome procrastination on your own, sometimes you are unable to notice the causes and keep repeating the same mistakes over and over again. The coach will be able to guide you in overcoming the subconscious resistance that causes you to procrastinate.

A coach can help you identify areas which you may be overlooking or unable to see because of what is called your blind spots. Sometimes no matter how obvious the answers may seem, people are unable to see these solutions because they tend to be hidden in their blind spots or overlooked.

Procrastination does not make you wrong or an incapable person in any way; it is a behaviour that was caused from past experiences. All behaviour can be modified at the subconscious level and this is where a coach can guide you in modifying that behaviour.

Remember that these are just indicators of your subconscious behaviour towards your conscious thoughts of your goals and dreams. This may not always be an accurate indication of what is really going on unconsciously. You will need to work with a graphologist for an accurate handwriting analysis of what your unconscious traits and habits may be. This is not absolutely necessary and is only an option you can take toward identifying what could be your unconscious blocks.

Consciously Changing Your Handwriting

However this does not mean that you cannot start writing out your goals and dreams right now. Despite what your unconscious responses may be, even if they are negative, if you write your goals and dreams out at the theta level of mind, chances are you will modify your behaviour subconsciously and will be able to achieve your goals and dreams.

Consciously changing your handwriting and practicing writing in straight lines can cause some subconscious behavioural changes for positive transformation. It will be like putting suggestions on your subconscious mind in the same way as self-hypnosis.

One option of enhancing your ability to subconsciously accept your goals and dreams is to write on sheets of paper with lines, practicing maintaining a straight line every time you write before writing down your actual goals and dreams.

Otherwise you can merely write your goals and dreams on paper with lines. As mentioned before; the best time to write out your goals and dreams is at night just before you go to sleep or in the morning when you have just woken up, this is the natural state of theta.

You do have another option of getting into theta as described in chapter ten "Accessing your theta level". However the time just before you go to sleep would probably be the most powerful time to write your goals and dreams, as you will fall asleep with those thoughts on your mind, allowing your subconscious mind to accept these new changes with relatively less resistance, which in turn will motivate you into taking action towards your goals and dreams, this is especially powerful for non-visual people.

Have a Structured Goal

Having a structured written goal enhances your thoughts and motivation around your goals on both the conscious and subconscious levels. Each goal should have its own structure and reviewed regularly to help you refine and restructure if necessary should there be obstacles that you are struggling to overcome.

This may seem like a lot of work initially and it probably will be depending on how big your goal may be, the important thing to remember that nothing comes easy because if it did, we would all have what we really want by now. Nothing can be achieved without some sacrifice and effort, think how rewarding and amazing you would feel once you have achieved your goal. To create a good structured goal, the following points must be kept in mind.

- Your goal must be written or stated in positive sentences or language. Do not be afraid to dream big. Be really specific about what it is that you really want?

- Write down where you are presently in terms of your life or your goal.

- Write down what your outcome will be. This means being specific with the outcome of the goal you are writing down. What will you see, hear and feel once you have achieved your goal? Write it the present tense as if you already have it.

- Write down what you think or how you will know when you have achieved your goal. Write it in the present tense specifying what you will see, hear and feel once you know you have achieved that goal. This is also an opportunity to add and further enhance what you have already written or are currently visualizing what the end result of achieving your goal will look like.

- Write down what you think or believe that achieving your goal or the outcome of the goal will give you and what it will allow you to do.

- Write down whether this goal is only for you or to be shared with others. Note if the goal you are trying to achieve is for others and not for you, chances are you will not achieve it or get the desired outcome. The important fact to remember is that you first have to help yourself before you can help others. Therefore it would be a good idea to write down how others could benefit from you achieving this goal even if the goal is only for you.

- Write down where and when this must happen, you can include the how if you already know how you will achieve the goal, most people don't know how they will achieve it, therefore most of the time it is important to focus on the end result and ask yourself "what do I have right now to get started"? You can also specify a person or people with whom you would like to achieve specific goals with.

- Write down the resources you have right now to get started with. Also write down what resources or things that you may need to get started and what will be required to achieve that goal. It is also a good idea, if you have never done something like this before, to try and identify or get into contact with people who have done something similar, this will help you build up knowledge, support and networks to help you achieve your goals.

- Ask yourself whether you are able to act as if you already have it? If the answer is no, what can you do or learn that could help you develop the ability to act as if you have already achieved that goal. This is important for overcoming subconscious resistance and obstacles that may block you from achieving those goals. It is a good idea to also write down how you can act as if you already achieved your goal.

- Finally take some time and really think about how achieving your goal will impact your life and how will your sacrifices affect others. Will it affect those around you in a positive or negative way? What options can you create that will get you the support of those around you and make it a positive experience for everyone? This is important as you want to avoid a situation where you start to alienate those closest to you. However it is also important to remember that sometimes or at some point you may find the need to move away from certain friends and co-workers especially if their negative attitudes are bringing you down and holding you back from achieving your goals.

When writing out your goals for the first time, avoid asking yourself whether it is right or wrong. The important thing is to get a first structure then look at it to see if you have been specific enough and that it is what you really want.

You may need to refine it and or restructure your goal until you see that it is written in the present tense and really describes what you really want and triggers positive emotions for you. The intention is to create a path of least resistance for your subconscious mind and to make it achievable on both the conscious and subconscious levels.

Once you have created this structure on the conscious or beta level, the next step is to re-write the goal on the theta level, just before you go to sleep. The following is an example of a written structured goal based on a person who wants to be a very successful life coach. You can use this example as a guideline or indication for writing and structuring your goals. Your written goal does not have to be an exact imitation of the following goal. It would be helpful to you to bring in your own creativity.

Example of a Written Structured Goal

First write out the intention of the goal; what is the goal? When would you like to achieve this goal?

I want to earn $4 million a year as an international life coach, teaching at seminars and workshops, as well as coaching in the area of mental performance with clients in the sports and business fields. I want to achieve this by the end of this year. (You can put in a specific date that is realistic to achieve e.g. a year from when you wrote this intention.)

The next step is to write out your current status. Where are you now? What do you currently earn? Also try and get a mental picture of what the gap is between what you currently earn and want to earn per year.

I am currently earning $75 thousand a year as a private life coach in the area of self-development and goal achievement. I only get to do one seminar every two months in my country. I feel stuck and believe that I am much more powerful than that and can do much better than what I am currently doing.

After you have made the intention of what you want and have specified where you are now, you write out the actual goal as if you already have it now.

I wake up each morning with a smile on my face and feelings of gratitude knowing that I do what I love to do most. My passion is my job. I have two seminars a month booked for the entire year in different parts of the world.

I successfully coach high profile clients in mental performance covering the areas that is important to them. I have a beautiful office in a building on the mountain side overlooking the city and beachfront. I receive calls daily from people who are excited to share their results and success from the coaching.

I love the fact that most of the people who come to my workshops and seminars around the world are referrals from people who have gained much success from my teachings and coaching. I love that I get new high profile clients on a regular basis referred to me by my existing clients.

I love working with the people I teach and coach and the greatest reward is seeing them succeed. I have a very effective website and a great marketing program. I am a member of a highly effective business networking group and I enjoy the opportunity of being able to speak to people every weekl about the services I offer. I love driving to my office in my new car and really enjoy the fact that I get to travel to different parts of the world to conduct my seminars, the fun part is that I now get to travel in business class and enjoy all the perks.

The above is just a short example of writing your goal in a specific way. However you can add even more detail like the type and colour of car you drive, the new house and its location and so forth. Be creative and just let your ideas flow.

This is also the part of the goal that you would re-write in the theta level, although I would recommend that you write everything from the intention to the end at the theta level to further enhance the subconscious mind to take the path of least resistance.

The next step is to take a good look at the goal that you have written and see if you are able to add more detail to make it even stronger on the subconscious level. If you already have put in a lot of detail, there is no need to add to the written goal.

You can further enhance your goal by writing in if possible the exact location of your new house or office like the suburb or area it is located in. Going right down to the street name if possible, (this part is not absolutely necessary but it will help in a number of ways). The important thing is to have the final outcome written out in as much detail as possible.

You can even add things like what the weather is like and other sights and sounds you might think you will be seeing. You can even go as far as specifying the amount you will earn each day or with each client. Maybe you might even want to write down how much money you have in the bank and what investments you may have, all of this written in the present tense.

Note when deciding on how much you want to earn per month or year, although you want the amount to be realistic, it's really about how much do you value yourself? If you put a low dollar amount down, ask yourself if you really see yourself as that small? Be kind to yourself and put high values because you deserve it.

If you want to further enhance your goal and make the outcome of that goal more appealing, it would be a good idea to write down what achieving your goal will allow you to do or possibly get for you.

- What else do you see that you can further achieve as a result from achieving your goal?
- Will it bring new opportunities?
- What are those possible opportunities?
- What new roles will you have in your business or work?

- Will it bring new contracts or allow you to expand your business?

- Will you have new friends or have the opportunity to make a difference in the world?

Remember that you are merely writing down possible opportunities that can arise from achieving your goal, therefore this does not have to be one hundred percent accurate as it is not possible to know what will happen in the future with certainty. Therefore just allow yourself to have fun with this and enjoy the process of your creativity and what you write.

Making Your Goal more Appealing

Based on the life coach goal above, here is an example of making the goal more appealing.

My life coaching profile and business has grown to such an extent that I am now a best-selling author. I appear regularly as a guest on various TV and Radio shows, I also have my own weekly Radio show and a weekly TV show, sharing ideas and creating opportunities for viewers to develop a healthy and meaningful lifestyle.

I am also playing my part in making a difference in this world by being part of two organizations, one that is involved in the conservation of endangered animals and the other organization working on projects that uplift humanity in many different ways. I love the idea that I get to serve humanity in this way and have a life that feels enlightened and fulfilled.

You may have written your goal down with as much detail and clarity as possible, however at this point it is important to get more clarity onto the subconscious mind on the purpose of the goal. This step requires that you write down for whom this goal is for? Is this goal only for you? Was this goal initiated by you, meaning was it your idea and you want to take this idea forward?

If the goal is not only for you, who else is involved and what are their roles in achieving this goal? Is the goal going to be maintained by you or are there going to be others helping you maintain that goal and what are their roles in the achievement of the goal?

Usually it is better to go with your idea because it usually is something you are passionate about. This does not make you selfish if the goal is only for you, it means you are following your heart and passion to achieve something you really want or love. Be clear with yourself that you are not creating a goal based on what someone else told you to do or what you could be, in this case there is likely to be a lack of follow through on achieving the goal.

There are times where you could become excited about what others tell you what you could be and you base your goals on that. You get caught up in the excitement of all of that because in that moment you may have not been open in knowing what you really want.

Over time you begin to realise that the goal you set is based on someone else's perception of you and it is not really an area you are passionate about and want to work in. Some people get caught up in the trap where they want to fulfil on someone else's dream, for example one or both of your parents may have struggled in life but they never got to fulfil on their dream of owning a particular business, even though it is done with love, the business venture or goal is based on the parents dream and not the individual's dream.

The consequence of this is that the individual does not get to realise his or her true potential, this does not necessarily mean that they are unsuccessful in the business. Therefore be very clear that the business is only for you or if there are others involved in that goal, that it is a goal you really want to achieve. Your passion will motivate you in the actions required to achieve that goal.

Reviewing your Goal

The next step is to review your goal ensuring that you are absolutely clear that it is what you really want, that you are clear on where and when you want to achieve that goal. If possible or necessary and you know how you can achieve that goal, you can add in the "how" and "with whom" if applicable at this point.

The purpose of the review is to allow for the opportunity to add more detail to the goal, maybe you left something out and need to add to it or to be absolutely clear that you have written exactly what you want. Take your time with this so as to be absolutely clear on your goal.

Creating the 'How'

You have probably heard many times "Don't worry about the how and when you will achieve your goal"; you are told to "Just focus on the end result". However nearly everyone does not know how they are going to achieve their end result and most importantly what actions they need to take.

There are a number of questions that you can write down to help you initiate the initial steps to create the "how" you will achieve that goal. The first thing is to look at what resources might be needed to achieve those goals? What do you have right now that could get you started on taking the actions to achieve those goals?

You don't have to have all the resources at hand, merely start with what you have and create the required resources as you move forward. There are three questions you can ask yourself to get started. Have you done this before? If the answer is yes, you will usually know what resources you need and where to get them.

If the answer is no, the next question is do you know someone who has done this before? A good idea at this point is to also write down a list of what you think you might need to achieve the successful outcome of the goal. You may not know everything that you may need, merely start the list and you can add to it as you move forward.

An Example of Creating the 'how'

The following is an example of creating the "how" based on the life coaching goal above.

I will contact a website designer to get my website designed and set up. I will also get someone to assist with my social media marketing as well as speak to marketing consultants on other best marketing options I can take. I will make a list of professional or very successful life coaches and start contacting them to see if any one of them would be willing to coach or mentor me as I start to build my business.

I will further enhance my skills by attending advanced seminars and workshops in my field. I will create and print flyers and business cards. I will do some research on pricing for my type of services and create packages that will be attractive to people who want to take up my coaching. I will make enquiries on business network groups in my area and join the best one for me.

This helps to create more clarity and motivate you into taking action especially when you write it down.

This is also very helpful for those who keep on asking the question "how will I get there?" It is also very helpful for non-visual people to create more clarity on their goals especially on the subconscious level to help overcome subconscious resistance on achieving the goal.

Once you have completed writing all of that down, it is important that you look at the goal again and ask yourself pertinent questions to be absolutely sure that this is the path for you to take.

- Firstly is achieving this goal good for you?

- Is it just good or for the greater good?

- Are there people around you that could be impacted or affected by you achieving your goal?

- How will achieving your goal be good for those around you?

- What will those around you stand to gain when you achieve your desired outcome?

- Is there anything they stand to lose by you achieving your goal?

It is good to take this time out and reflect on how you could affect those around you when working towards achieving your goal. This does not mean you have to stop working on your goal but will give you the opportunity to re-structure your goal so that it will also benefit those around you.

When you take the time to reflect on this and those around you, it will also give you the opportunity to identify how you can get those around you or loved ones involved in your goals, helping to reduce the risk of you being consumed in your goal and causing unnecessary relationship problems with those around you. This will help you identify how you can achieve your goal successfully with relative harmony.

The above goal example and structure of the goal was derived from a structure of neuro linguistic programing (NLP) "Creating an achievable outcome". NLP was founded and developed by John Grinder a professor of linguistics and psychologist Richard Bandler. This is probably one of the best goal structures that could help prevent subconscious resistance and make achieving your goals much stronger and easier.

Non-visual people should try and read through their written goals at least two or three times a day, for at least thirty days, to help motivate them to be in action both consciously and subconsciously in achieving their desired outcome. I personally use this goal structure and also teach it in my NLP practice. It is also a good idea to review your goals regularly to identify where changes or restructuring of the goal may be required.

Remember you won't always achieve one hundred percent of what you imagine or visualize your outcome will be, no one can be certain about the future. The important thing is to look at what you have now to get started. Once you get started it becomes easier as you move forward.

From time to time you will face obstacles, see it as part of the process rather than a mountain in your way. This will help keep you calm and find a way around those obstacles. An important thing to keep in mind is that to avoid comparing where you are now with your desired outcome or how much more you have to achieve to get there, avoid measuring the gap between where you are and the end result.

A good idea is to look how far you have come from when you first started and celebrate that. There will be times when you may not achieve some goals completely but will get very close to where you wanted to be in the first place. Constantly comparing where you are now and how much further you still have to go to achieve your goal could cause frustration and lead you to give up on achieving that goal.

Another thing to avoid is becoming attached to the desired outcome, this could cause you to fail at achieving the goal or in other areas of your life, and it could also cause relationships to breakdown. Know your outcome and focus on the actions you want to take without any expectations.

Expectations could lead to disappointments. The important thing is not whether you will fail or succeed but how far you get and most important having fun getting there. Follow your passion and success will follow you.

Final Word

One of the greatest inspirations and influences on my life was the life story of Hellen Keller. I remember watching the movie of Helen Keller's life, "The Miracle Worker", for the first time at age seventeen. It deeply moved me, however still being a teenager I did not take note of the role and gift that Anne Sullivan played in Hellen Keller's life.

For those of you who are unaware of who Hellen Keller is or who have not watched the movie or read the book, Hellen Keller was born on June 27 1880. She was born as a healthy child but at nineteen months developed an unknown illness that left her deaf and blind. Hellen Keller despite being deaf and blind grew up to be one of the greatest influences on life in the area of education of blind and visually impaired people around the world.

She was one of the greatest activists of human and women's rights during the early to mid-nineteen hundreds. She became one of the top journalists and authors of her time. She also had a lot of influence in the political arena and met many presidents of various countries throughout her lifetime. Hellen Keller received many accolades, awards as well as doctorates from various universities around the world. Hellen Keller passed away on June 1 1968.

I had watched the movie a number of times over the years and every time was moved by it. It was not until 2010 while watching the movie did I start to take notice of Anne Sullivan, Hellen's teacher and to some extent guardian. Until the age of six, Hellen Keller had no existence other than her physical existence. There was no sight and sound causing her to become quite a wild child and causing stress within the household. It was only when Hellen met Anne in March 1887 did Helen's life change. Anne Sullivan visually impaired herself, created a whole new way of communicating with Helen that made Helen the famous person she was.

Anne Sullivan used the language of touch to teach Hellen to read and write which gave Hellen existence and a voice. Observing this aspect while watching that movie in 2010 awakened my fascination with language – the language of the subconscious mind. Helen Keller had no recognition or memory of her life before Anne Sullivan came into her life because there was no language to describe it. Her memories of her life before age six are only those told to her about her life during that time. It was only when Anne Sullivan gave Helen that gift of language, did Hellen start to experience real existence.

In my personal view Anne Sullivan was a true life hero as much as Helen Keller was. Anne was able to influence life and existence through the language of touch. It was then did I realise that the subconscious mind could respond to various forms of language.

Language for the subconscious mind can be found in all of the five senses of human beings. Since 2010 I also started observing how language could influence the subconscious mind to modify behaviour through hypnosis. Over a period of six years I would observe clients and their use of their own internal language to identify how their spoken words, whether internally or externally was influencing the way they took action in achieving their objectives and goals.

I wanted to understand why I and so many people like me who had done various courses, attended seminars on self-development were not achieving much. I wanted to know why these various techniques were not working. As a hypnotherapist I was able to observe how the subconscious mind would resist change and how it was so easy to fall back into those old habits and behaviours. During the past six years while putting the material together for this book, I continued to attend various seminars and online courses on self-development so that I could observe my own subconscious resistance.

During this time I would observe how language would influence my emotions and the way I did things or behaved in this world. I noticed just how easy it was to fall back into that automatic mode making it so difficult to cause those positive transformations. I would also observe just how easy it was to allow ourselves to be influenced by the perceptions of others and what we would call external factors.

There were times when I would purposefully use negative language on myself and observe the emotions it caused. The one fact that I discovered is that it caused me to have high resistance to any coaching or teachings of other workshops and seminars that I attended.

I also resisted the power of self-love despite teaching it to my clients. I saw how self-love and forgiveness greatly influence positive transformation in my clients but still found that I was resisting it. I continued to resist

211

this self-love until the day I changed the language around it going on in my mind. I quickly discovered what an important role language played in the way we existed in this world.

There is no existence without language in any form. Language influences the way everything in life is created or the outcomes that occur in life. When working with Neuro Linguistics programming I was able to see how language had a tendency to be a self-fulfilling prophecy in people's lives as well as my own. I was able to observe just how language was the creation of all that exists.

The concept of Chapter One, The Essence of You, was derived from understanding how language played a role in giving Hellen Keller existence as well as a personal experience that I had. I found that when I was able to clear my mind completely in meditation, going to a place where nothing exists including me, from this place of nothing, a new language could be created for positive transformation.

I found creating this new language in this way, I was able to greatly influence the modifying of my old habits and behaviours with little resistance. I would then use guided meditation with my clients to help them create this new language and saw how it transformed their lives with less resistance.

You do not have to be in meditation to change your language. You can start by using powerful words on yourself and you will realise just how easy it is to change emotions. Like language, where you have the choice to change your language to influence positive trans-formation, you have that choice to decide how you want to feel. Feelings and emotions in any given moment is a choice. It usually is triggered unconsciously from past events and memories despite feeling it in the present moment.

We have all been programmed to believe that emotions are caused from external situations. However this is only an unconscious trigger. When we say things like "that situation makes me feel bad" or "he/she makes me feel so small", the reality is that nothing and nobody can make you feel the way you do. Your feelings are within you and you have the control on how you want to feel. This unconscious belief that our feelings or emotions actually come from outside events or actions of people, is the barrier that prevents us from breaking through those subconscious resistance.

Looking back at my own life and the struggles that I have been through, from financial to relationships, almost every aspect of my life, I have been able to discover how language and the unwillingness to take control of my emotions have played a role in the many years of struggle. It was not easy to accept that I was the cause of this life and made some really bad decisions along the way. As well as ruin some very good relationships. When I was able to notice how I played the victim, I woke up to a new reality.

I was one of those who snubbed those who spoke of positive thinking, as well as throwing up my hands claiming that self-help techniques do not work. The truth is even in the past six years, despite working with clients and seeing their success, I still found myself resisting the change and challenges facing me. It was so much easier to teach others than to apply it to myself. It was only when I started applying my own techniques that I taught others, did my life truly transform in almost every aspect of my life.

I quickly realised that all the self-help techniques, books and seminars actually do work; it is our own internal language and subconscious resistance that makes it not work. As I discovered more and more in depth how language played a role in how we decide our outcomes, I was able to better understand the power of being responsible for my own life.

No matter what our circumstances, whether we believe we are right or wrong, or whether we have had a difficult life or not, the hard truth is that until we stop playing the victim and start being responsible for our outcomes and life, we will never discover how powerful we really are.

Over the years I realised just how important positive thinking really is. It is so important to work at being positive both emotionally and mentally at all times if we are really going to make any significant changes in our own lives. It is not just about ignoring the negative parts, we first have to acknowledge and accept the negative before we can start to make any change. We then have to take responsibility for whatever is negative in our life before we can start to create the change we desire for a better life.

Once we have taken that responsibility, there has to be a willingness to detach emotionally from it and completely let go. Positive transformation takes courage and strength and a strong desire and willingness to want to cause that change. I wrote this book to describe that responsibility and that it is all based in language. I did not write this book to promise you an instant magical life that will suddenly appear.

I wanted to tell the truth, and that is there is no quick fix in life. Positive thinking alone is not going to change anything much. There has to be a willingness on your

214

part to want that change and be able to do what it takes to make that change. I am not going to pretend that it is so easy to transform your life. It is not going to be easy at all, transforming yourself has to start within; it is going into self that is going to be the hardest journey you will ever experience. This is where the courage comes in.

Dealing with oneself and accepting the ugly bits as well is not going to be easy. This book is written in a way for you to discover yourself in a slow yet steady process. This is not about me giving you all the answers because all those answers exist within you anyway. The aim is to slowly guide you to that point where you will discover your own internal language. It is from here where you can start to powerfully create that new life you really want.

Don't be in a hurry. Take your time with this and really try and discover who you really are. Right now most of your personality and traits are based in what others thought you should be. You like almost all human beings have defined who you really are based on external factors.

Now is the time to re-define who you really are. It is not about what others are doing, what is going on in the world around you; it is about you defining who you want to be and who you really are. Now is the time to take the journey within to unlock all those secrets of who you really are and just how unique you are in this world.

Be patient with yourself and be willing to deal with yourself in ways you have never done before. Start with two or three kind words about yourself each day and build it up from there. As you start to discover your power, it will no longer matter what others think or say. You will start to define who you really are and realise that with effort and persistence, you will be able to create the life you really want.

This is a journey so no matter how difficult it may get, allow yourself to enjoy the ride there. It will all be worth it in the end and that is the one and only promise that I can truly offer you.

Life is too good to stop now.

Mo Khalpey

About the Author

Mo Khalpey is an Author, life coach, hypnotherapist, NLP practitioner and teacher specialising in coaching self-empowerment, defining and focusing on goals, creating your life plan, developing confidence and self-expression in achieving your goals and dreams.

Mo also specialises in the area of mind coaching for sports performance and performance arts. Mo does not use hypnosis in his coaching but rather teaches techniques to overcome stress, and meditation to achieve goals faster, proving that when you train your mind first, your body and everything else follows.

Mo's interest in meditation started more than 15 years ago through his fascination with the human mind. This fascination led him to study hypnosis and hypnotherapy to better understand how the subconscious mind works and why people struggle so much at living the life of their dreams.

This scientific approach has been the foundation in the development of Mo's meditation teachings which is based on a self-hypnotic form of creating the habit of achieving goals, confidence, self-expression and fulfilling dreams deep into the subconscious mind.

These coaching techniques combine the power of visualisation with the art of language to better understand when self-sabotage and subconscious resistance is taking place, stopping one from achieving their goals.

Mo has been on a personal journey facing many difficult challenges in relationships, finance, achieving goals and being connected to other human beings, including living with a visual disability. The many years of studying the human mind and human behaviour, has led him to develop techniques that helped him overcome those difficult challenges. Mo has spent 16 years of his life studying, practicing and developing various techniques to create the unique set of techniques he uses in his coaching today.

Mo is the author of the book "Aistiq Meditations: A scientific approach to achieving goals"[1]. This is an easy reading book describing how the mind works and the methodologies in a step by step guide that helped him and many others achieve their dreams.

Mo has also studied how language affects the mind both in a positive and negative way, using this understanding combined with NLP techniques. Mo has coached many people to achieve their desired outcome in a quicker and more simplified manner.

Mo's unique teachings have helped thousands of people achieve their goals and create a stress free life for themselves. Today through the Aistiq centre Mo offers a series of workshops and seminars, as well as coaching individuals to create a better lifestyle and empower themselves. Mo also offers mental coaching for sports performance and performance arts developed from his training in hypnosis and sports.

1   Kima Global Publishers 2015

Lightning Source UK Ltd.
Milton Keynes UK
UKOW04f1915031017
310355UK00001B/51/P